WHAT ARE WORDS WORTH?

Pete May

For Nicola, Lola and Nell

CONTENTS

ACKNOWLEDGMENTS

Firstly thanks to James McConnachie for publishing my feature 'Diary of a Writing Nobody' in *The Author*, the journal of the Society of Authors. That article gave me the inspiration to complete the year-long diary of a writer grappling with the gig economy and working from home long before it became normal.

Also thanks to Caroline Sanderson for interviewing me for the 'My Writing Life' spot in *ALCS News* after which it felt like I had become the poster boy for poorly-paid writers. Outing myself as broke might not have been a great way of impressing agents and publishers, but that piece did receive a lot of messages of solidarity from the writing community and brought home the fact that it's increasingly difficult for a wordsmith who isn't a bestseller to earn a living.

Big thanks to typeface guru Andrew Chapman — whom I've known since the 1980s — for his great cover design. I'd also like to thank my family for putting up with the writer in their midst: my wife and fellow writer Nicola Baird for advice and inspiration, Lola May for proof-reading and Nell May for early page-reading and allowing me to document her teenage years.

Hopefully this book will make some people laugh, but also deliver a few serious points. The only time I've ever delivered jam today for my family was when I wrote about visiting the Wilkin & Sons preserves factory in Tiptree, Essex and received some free samples. But my name has appeared on a few book spines and that's what keeps us authors going.

What are words worth? I'll leave it up to you the reader to decide.

Pete May, October 2020

WHAT ARE WORDS WORTH?

JANUARY 2019

BEING BROKE — COULD HAVE BEEN A
CONTENDER — DRILL RAP — IN FOR A
FIVERR —THE WOOD MAN COMETH — DEATH
AS A UNIQUE SELLING POINT —WAITING FOR
THE GIFT OF SOUND AND VISION — PARK
LIFE COACH

Tuesday, January 1 2019

Another year arrives and I am still what is termed a midlist writer. It's a polite industry expression for writers who aren't bestsellers. As a midlist author I have published 15 books. I have delivered manuscripts on time, hopefully enjoy a reputation for competence and have a small but dedicated set of readers who like my work. Most authors are midlist — and thankfully there doesn't seem to be a term for bottom-of-the-list writers, unless it's bottomlist.

But the thing is it's getting harder and harder for midlist authors to survive. If you don't sell you don't get advances any more. If a publisher doesn't pay a big advance they don't put money into marketing a book or a large print run. Back in 2008 I received an advance of £15,000 (minus ten per cent for the agent) for my book *There's a Hippo in my Cistern*. Now I'm writing for just royalties. Publishers no longer want to nurture writers in the hope that they will eventually have a breakthrough book. They want either best-sellers, or young photogenic debut authors they can tout as the next publishing sensation.

I've also spent much of my life working as a journalist and that source of income is drying up too as newspapers and magazines cut their freelance budgets. Increasingly people expect me to write or talk for nothing in return for a book plug. Until recently there was my part-time job as an associate lecturer in Sports Journalism that brought in around £4k a year for 12 years, but last year I was made redundant.

For the past 20 years my income has been declining. In contrast to my peers who are receiving ever-larger salaries commensurate with their experience. In my peak income year of 1997-98 I was earning £22k pa from freelance writing. In 2013-14 I was still making £7k in self-employed income. But last year my freelance turnover was just under £3000, although I had been writing my book *Man About Tarn,* which has now been published and might claw back a little income.

Yet in many ways I'm tremendously lucky being paid to do something I enjoy. Many people dream of being published and never get anywhere close. I've got to see my name on a book spine and that's priceless. I've managed to earn a living from words for most of my life.

Nor am I going to plead poverty. When my parents died in 2007 they left me enough money to pay off our mortgage. I've got enough of their money left in the building society to keep me going for the next ten years if necessary, although it's being depleted year on year. There's even a small pension. When I was 55 I cashed in my private pension, mainly because I couldn't afford to contribute to it anymore. So each month I now receive £43 after tax, which works out at £657 a year. Not much, but something. Though yes, it would be nice to earn more than I am spending.

Why do I keep writing? Rather like supporting West

Ham, it's the hope that keeps me going, even if it's more often despair that grips me. Like most midlist writers I know that for all their feigned expertise, no-one in the publishing industry really has any idea of what sells. The unlikeliest of ideas can catch the imagination of the reading public. Luck can turn. And really just getting a book published is a triumph in itself. It's also a matter of professional pride. Rejection comes all the time for authors, from agents, publishers and reviewers, so there's a tremendous sense of achievement in proving the doubters wrong. Somehow money earned from writing seems much more worthwhile than any of my other forms of income.

And I'm not a no-hoper. I've had more than a hundred pieces published in the *Guardian*, written book reviews for the *Independent*. My features on football and Greatest Living Englishmen appeared in *Loaded* when it was the publishing sensation of the 1990s. For a decade I was the gossip columnist on *Time Out*, writing the Sidelines section. For a similar period I was the weekly London Spy columnist on *Midweek* and my quotes appeared in adverts on the London Underground under the heading of 'free thinking'.

Besides, last November I gained literary immortality — admittedly for being poorly paid. *ALCS News*, the online newsletter of the Authors Licensing and Collecting Society, printed an interview where I outed myself as earning a rubbish income from a 'portfolio' career of writing books, journalism, teaching, blogging, talks, PR and renting out a room in my house. The interview was by Caroline Sanderson, who coincidentally did the publicity at Penguin for my first ever published book, *The Lad Done Bad*, co-written with Denis Campbell and Andrew Shields. In the interview I commented that I could probably earn more moving books around

Amazon's warehouse rather than writing my own. There were many supportive tweets from other writers.

I'm not sure that revealing I'm skint is a great way of enticing agents and publishers. Still, I don't much care anymore. Publishers' profits are up and the Society of Authors reckons authors receive three per cent of publishers' turnover, with shareholders getting three times the income of people who create the books. By squeezing the creators, the industry risks destroying itself.

But there's also an inkling of an idea in this. I've been freelance for 32 years, I'm now 59 and I'm not going to be told that I'm not a writer. For the next year I'm going to keep a diary of just what it takes to survive as a freelance wordsmith.

Wednesday January 2
After yesterday's bank holiday it's back to work in front of my Mac. My Kindle Direct Publishing (KDP) account reveals that I have sold one copy of my book on the Lake District, *Man About Tarn*, making me a profit of £1.73 from the sale price of £2.99. A quick check of Google's AdSense reveals that my West Ham blog has made a whole 2p in advertising revenue.

Let me introduce you to my work hub. My kingdom is here at the back of our Victorian house in London. The office is in the L-shaped extension that was built on the back of our house ten years ago.

It's not quite *World of Interiors*. I have a desk area in the narrow corridor next to the French windows. A metre from my wonky swivel chair — I must try to fix it — is a door into the downstairs loo and shower. When our lodger Rosie stays for two nights a week I try not to work in the evenings, as she needs access to the bathroom and probably doesn't want me listening outside.

There's a window in front of my desk and from here I

can see our wintry garden. A chicken shed stands in the far corner, which houses Margaret Hatcher and Egg Miliband, our ageing and increasingly non-laying Bantams. The garden has a small pond and a wooden swing that our children are too old to use, though the young girls next door often make illicit trips over the fence to play on it. There are my wife Nicola's numerous pots of unspecified plants, a collapsing wooden table, an out of control privet hedge and lots of wood chippings on the ground where once there was grass — children and chickens soon removed it.

I survey my office area; my 'chicken shoes' for mucking out the coop are stored beneath my mum and dad's 1980s TV stand; there's a tray of metal objects such as broken coffee makers and bits of toasters which we intend to recycle some day; theatre programmes, tax files, a bucket, an ironing board, a ladder, my daughter Nell's bike, gardening equipment, Essex tourist board literature, a storm lamp; a pile of *Guardian Weekend* magazines; Nicola's riding boots; a wicker basket of ancient Wellington boots; the pieces of Victorian pottery I found in the spoil of road works outside; two fold-up summer chairs; an empty Celebrations chocolate box; a large roll of lino; two printer ink cartridges; and a pile of 1980s diaries. Marie Kondo could probably get a whole TV series out of this.

Nicola has her office at the front of the house in what is also our library. She has a desk surrounded by teetering mounds of letters, papers, jars of snacks and a box of Islington Faces canvas bags. Here she works on *The Pavement*, a magazine for homeless people, and also her blog Islington Faces, as well as teaching media studies at the London College of Communication. Nicola's written books such as *The Estate We're In* on car culture, *Homemade Kids* on bringing up children and the eco handbook *Save Cash and Save the Planet*. But like me she's not become rich through her literary endeavours. She also teaches at a riding school in Trent Park one day a week and paddle boarding at the boat club on the canal during the summer months. We both have portfolio careers, only Nicola's portfolio is bigger than mine.

We met at the *New Statesman* back in 1993. I was sub-editing two days a week and she was co-ordinating the campaign to fight John Major's libel action against the magazine. Nicola spent ten years working at Friends of the Earth on their magazine *Earthmatters* and is a passionate environmentalist.

Since we bought our house in 2004 we've put in solar panels, double-glazing and a grass roof in a bid to be sustainable. The only thing we can't do is declutter. We don't have a car and only fly once a decade. She is full of fire and always planning something; while I like to relax in front of the TV watching *Doctor Who* with a beer. But our relationship seems to work as I force her to relax sometimes and she takes me out of my comfort zone.

We have two daughters. Nell is 17 and taking her A levels at sixth-form college. She's studying hard at History, Politics, English and *Love Island* — and is also discovering the joys of going out with her friends, hanging out at 'Prim' (Primrose Hill) and other teenage wastelands. She is better at night than in the mornings. For some reason she still seems to lose control of her limbs at the table and requires me to pour out her water, cut her toast, find the Marmite and many other tasks. But then I am only staff.

This year Nell will hopefully be leaving for university and Nicola is very worried about the prospect of no children at home. Saying that we can watch lots of *Doctor Who* and first generation *Star Trek* DVDs doesn't seem to soothe her much.

My older daughter Lola is now 20 and a student studying International Relations at SOAS (the School of Oriental and African Studies) in London. Inspired by a love of Victor Hugo and *Les Miserables* she spent a year in Paris after her A levels, working as a nanny and getting a French childcare qualification.

She now lives in a student house at Turnpike Lane, so she's able to come for family dinners on Mondays and also works in a nearby café one day a week. Lola has been a French revolutionary since watching *Les Miserables*, and after being a Corbynite activist is now more anarchic but is still picketing on behalf of striking lecturers; although looking at the five different sorts of coffee-makers in her house her collective seems quite capable of being a bit bohemian too. She often confuses me with words like cisgen and bougie.

Her empty bedroom upstairs is used for guests and sometimes lodgers; though her shelves of eclectic books, from Virgil and Homer to *Game of Thrones, 1000 Years of Annoying the French* and *Lord of the Rings,* make it seem as if she's almost still here.

So that's our gang. Plus there's Rosie who stays two nights a week. She has her own place in Norwich, but works four days a week for an arts fair in London. She stays on Mondays and Tuesdays, parking her bike in the front room and sleeping on the sofa bed. She was warned in the advert Nicola placed that our house is never tidy and seems pretty good-humoured about our chaotic family life.

The final member of our household is Vulcan the border terrier. It's good to have another male in the house and Vulcan is similar to most men. He doesn't want to talk about feelings, which is good. Vulcan likes food, sleep and to aggressively patrol the garden tilting against Joe the cat from next door, a family of urban foxes and rogue squirrels. He once took hallucinogenic drugs at the Standon Calling festival, having somehow eaten someone's stash, and spent the night at the vet's, having keeled over. We thought he might die, but he recovered and produced a great concept album on wizards and dragons. I wrote about this incident in the *Guardian*, so like the rest of my family he's good for copy.

Tuesday, January 3

My morning duties start. I release the chickens from their fox-proof inner coop, muck them out and scatter some seed while making clucking noises. Rather like Marlon Brando in *On The Waterfront* talking to his pigeons, I am now befriending fowl, reassuring myself that I could have been a contender. Vulcan the border terrier rushes out into the garden barking at possible squirrels, cats, foxes and assorted garden intruders. Then he squats down to do a poo on the wood chips, which I then pick up on a shovel and flush down the loo.

This is the year I have to try and earn more money to take the financial pressure off Nicola and to cope with what will be an expensive 12 months. We're invited to Sarlat in France this summer to celebrate Nicola's mum Fiona's 80th birthday, which will entail a lot of expense in fares. It's my 60th birthday coming up in August and my sister is arriving from Australia for four weeks, which will also involve a series of mini-breaks. We will also plan to take a family holiday and I'm planning on visiting the Lake District several times to try and complete walking all 214 Wainwright fells and then write about the experience. Add to this the fact that Nell is going off Inter-Railing and we may well experience Mr Micawber's "difficulties of a pecuniary nature."

It's time to log on to the KDP website. Three copies of *Man About Tarn* sold today, two in paperback, one e-book, reveals my sales bar chart. *Man About Tarn* is 39,948 in the Amazon Kindle chart and 269,225 in the Amazon paperback chart. I click on Blogger in a new tab. My *Hammers in the Heart* West Ham blog has made 5p in advertising revenue through AdSense. Every little helps.

I have a near-victory dealing with a national newspaper – a rejection for my feature idea, but at least they acknowledge my email. Adding my CV at the end of the email seems to have helped. Bludgeon them round the head with my 15 books.

The doorbell rings and some dog food arrives. An hour later another trill of the bell – two bags of wood chippings that Nicola has ordered for the garden. I sign an electronic device with my finger. Should I be a van driver, I wonder? They seem to get lots of assignments. Nicola's friend Kimi has recommended checking out copywriting jobs via an online agency. But do I want to be "demonstrating best practice in the Group values, mission and vision?" I am a maverick! Thirty-one years a freelancer! A free spirit!

Wednesday January 4
Pick up a number of burger containers and KFC chip packets that the local fox has left in our garden. The urban fox now ignores our real life chickens in favour of the fast food variety. In the middle of the night we often hear the foxes leaping on and off our bike shed, shrieking and generally having a feral party.

A plumber calls at the door to attend to a dripping tap that has been annoying my wife. He discovers there's no isolation valve in the bathroom. Perhaps there's no isolation valve for freelance writers either. Which is why I have joined the gig economy on Fiverr. I'm offering to come up with book titles for authors who realise the pun is mightier than the sword. After all, people seemed to like my own titles – *Man About Tarn*, *Goodbye to Boleyn*, *The Joy of Essex*. Those in the know say the idea is to start cheaply and get some good reviews, then increase prices. My first job earned a five-star review, even though the $5 fee, after Fiverr took its cut, amounted to just £3. So I've upped my price to $15. If this is the gig economy then I'm bottom of the bill in the crash-out tent at Glastonbury.

Tuesday January 5
The doorbell rings. It's Terry the slightly lairy window cleaner. We find it hard to say no to him. Nicola gets to the door first. "Alright darling, how you doing, do you want these windows cleaning, they're filthy!" he says. I'm not sure they are that dirty, but he seems to treat us an unofficial cashpoint whenever he needs money. Terry and his nephew get to work with buckets and sponges. We're £60 down and make a trip to the cash point.

My mobile rings. It's my doctor. Last year I had a health scare after contracting a urine infection. My blood test results have come in and the news is that my PSA level is much reduced, meaning I don't have prostate cancer, which is splendid.

My doctor is German and not dissimilar to Jurgen Klopp. When he enthusiastically suggested a physical examination of my prostate last year, I kept imagining it was Jurgen with his gloved hand in unusual places, probably saying that everything was "cool". It wasn't the sort of *gegenpressing* I had ever envisaged. It also seemed quite an apt metaphor for what the print and publishing industries have been doing to writers…

Sunday January 6
More health MOTs. Today I leave out my contact lens in

preparation for my second cataract operation. After a successful cataract operation on my left eye last year, I've been wearing just one contact lens in my right eye. Now that lens has to be left out as part of the pre-op preparation.

At 59 I could have waited longer for the cataracts to be removed. But the mistiness in my vision was restricting my ability to see West Ham games — although that isn't always a bad thing. The first operation was a success and my optician says it is sensible to get both eyes operating at the same level — even if there is a one in a thousand risk of something going wrong and possible blindness.

One alternative is to wear a pair of glasses with just one lens in them. Only with one eye at minus 10 and the other at minus 0.5, the effect is like a headache-inducing hallucinogenic trip, perhaps like the one Vulcan experienced when he overdosed at the Standon Calling festival. So I opt for no glasses, working with one good eye and hoping the bad eye will eventually adjust. The dizziness can't be any worse than that induced by dealing with commissioning editors with zero budgets. And as a freelancer in the new gig economy, like a 1970s footballer, you play on through injury.

Monday, January 7
My eyes seem to be adjusting a little with the stronger eye dominating the weaker. Sold an e-book and made £1.73 on KDP. My blog has made 21p on AdSense. An agent responds to my ideas. He cites Raynor Winn's *The Salt Path* as a book that has a USP, in that Winn and her husband have lost their home and received a terminal diagnosis as they walk the south west coast path. The best I can do is a problem with bruxism (the grinding of teeth), a slightly enlarged prostate, and a cataract operation. The

agent adds that he really has to fall in love with every book he takes on. That line again. Is it just coincidence that agents only fall in love with books that make them large amounts of money?

Thursday January 10

At my desk for 9.30am, accompanied by the sound of drilling on the rear extension being built by our neighbours. They have been considerate keeping us informed about their plans, but it's inevitably going to involve a few weeks of noise. Rampant foxes have left a trail of burger wrappers across our back garden. I give up and walk the dog, then read the paper in order to keep up with the currency of ideas. It's good to see Brexit is going so well... nice work, Theresa. I return to my desk to compete with more pneumatic drilling and workmen walking on the grass roof above my office.

Most of the afternoon is spent redoing the cover of my old book *Flying So High* for the paperback version on KDP. I've discovered how to add a spine and back cover blurb. Much of my life is spent curating my own work.

Frank Turner's song *The Ballad of Me and My Friends* starts to play in my head: "None of this is going anywhere..." So I play it on iTunes and then my computer takes me to several other songs with Ballad in the title, *The Ballad of Mott the Hoople*, *The Ballad of John and Yoko* and *The Ballad of a Well-Known Gun*. It's very easy to get distracted working from home.

A call from Ben Bradman. He used to edit a magazine that I wrote for, but now works in the world of PR and branding ideas. Ben has asked me to do a day's work helping to rebrand a company. But for this assignment first I have to scan and return a confidentiality agreement. I think Stormy Daniels once signed something similar. There's no sleaze involved here, but lots of confidential business information, "written and oral, that could cause injury to the client if disclosed". The agreement contains three sides of verbiage. I suspect that I have signed away my children and at least one testicle. Is it going over to the dark side working in PR? Well, I need the £150.

Friday January 11
It's quite enjoyable spending the day brainstorming names that project reliability, trustworthiness and accuracy. Maybe I should invent one for myself.

Saturday January 12
Head over to my old pal Vicky's birthday party at a Vauxhall bar. Nicola is impressed by the Thames-side venue. It's nice to be among journalists discussing ideas rather than alone at home.

Jackie has started a website with Ruby offering words to go and is also doing some financial journalism. Dee is now at Transport for London's in-house magazine. Jo is completing the work of her late partner. Vicky was once editor of *Time Out* and *Inside Soap*, among other mags. She is now working for a cruising magazine (nautical not gay) having left her previous high-pressure job. Nicola is able to show all the drinking journos a copy of *The Pavement* magazine, though there are no big projects for me to announce. But perhaps like the Dexys Midnight Runners' sleeve notes said, I'm lying low waiting for the big one.

Monday January 14
A Fiverr order arrived yesterday and I have two days to complete it. A clock ticks down from 48 hours on Fiverr's site, rather like something from a Bond movie. For this 'gig' (I guess it sounds more rock'n'roll than low-paid assignment) a man from Leeds wants a title for

his bodybuilding book. I spend a couple of hours going through prospective titles and exchange some emails to establish exactly what he wants. He likes what I've come up with. In a couple of weeks I should be around £9 better off. But I'm helping other writers, and earning anything feels better than nothing.

Tuesday January 15
Off to Moorfields hospital for my pre-op assessment, which takes two hours. The subsidence man arrives to monitor the cracks that have appeared in our Victorian house. As in Jarndyce and Jarndyce, the insurers will be making a judgement soon.

I perform my morning routine of checking book sales on KDP, but no copies sold. Another agent isn't impressed by my midlist track record.

But there's a boost too – a review of my book *Man About Tarn* in *Country Walking* magazine. The headline reads, "Is this the best book title of the year?" A plug in Britain's top-selling walking magazine should improve sales. It might only end up making £1000 for a year's work, but I've wanted to write about the Lake District for 20 years and it's something I'm proud of.

The magazine has also reproduced short extracts from my book covering caterpillars on Skiddaw, vandalism of the Robinson Mitchell statue in Cockermouth, dodgy Trip Adviser reviews, the joy of walking alone, sunset at Wasdale and the walker's sense of freedom in the fells.

Wednesday January 16
A pile of wood appears on the doorstep. We have a phantom wood giver, whom I call the Wood Man. Ten years ago we had a green open house day and he noted that we had a wood burner. Ever since he's been leaving offcuts from his DIY activities. He never stops to check if

we want the wood. Our cellar is full of more than we can burn. I take another bundle down into our stockpile

One of our neighbours, who works in TV, tells me he saw the piece on my low income travails in *ALCS News*. It's a kind of fame, I guess, adjusting to my new poverty chic status.

We need to prepare a bed for our new second lodger. Rosie is still staying two nights in the living room, but despite my misgivings about becoming a latter-day Rigsby from *Rising Damp*, Nicola has insisted we need another lodger. So we have recruited Monica, a hospital psychologist from Sussex, who will occupy Lola's bedroom for two nights a week. My house earns more than me now.

A glance at the newsagents reveals a further traducing of my surname. I take a picture of the *Daily Express's* headline "DISMAY" emblazoned over a picture of PM Theresa. "She valiantly fought for her deal but suffered a crushing defeat by 230 votes." Circulate the picture on Facebook and get 20 likes and seven comments.

Read *Normal People* by Sally Rooney in the theatre café, trying to keep up with the zeitgeist. Basically two students make cups of tea and can't decide whether to go out with each other for 200 pages. It's a good coming of age story, though somewhat over-hyped by the press. I look up from my Americano to observe two actors discussing working class life in the window seat while a woman has a life coaching session on the next table. Life is becoming like a Sally Rooney novel.

Monica the new lodger arrives and seems quite self-reliant. She prefers to shower and leave the house before seven am and stays in her room for the evening. Nicola has her photographer friend Kimi over for dinner. They are planning their forthcoming Islington Faces exhibition at Islington Museum. Nicola discusses her project while balancing on a curved beam that the Wood Man has left. It acts like a giant see-saw and is apparently good for increasing her core strength when paddle-boarding starts again in the summer.

As Kimi leaves we discover more wood has appeared on the doorstep from the mysterious Wood Man. Our wood stockpile could be useful once society goes a bit *Mad Max* after Brexit and there are rampaging mobs on the Seven Sisters Road.

Friday January 18

It's an early start as I have to be in at Moorfields Hospital at 7.30am for my cataract operation. There is a lot of hanging around. A large arrow is drawn above my eye in marker pen - a simple but old school method of ensuring they get the correct eye. At 11am I'm finally given a local anaesthetic lying on a trolley with a cover over my face. The scary part is that I lose all vision in my eye and have no idea if it will return until the next morning when the staff remove the bandage.

My good eye is covered with a blindfold. During the operation I can hear the disembodied voices of the surgeons and feel a little poking of the eye, but nothing painful, just a lot of water washing over my eye. It's best to keep calm and concentrate on the patterns I can see in my eye. When it's all over my eye is covered in a pad and bandage.

Afterwards there's a cup of tea and a sandwich. Then Nicola arrives to take me home. Only she has found a mulberry tree in the Moorfields St Ann's grounds. She has picked some berries and arrived in the waiting room covered with red stains all over her hands, looking like a particularly incompetent eye surgeon after a bout of eye-gouging worthy of *King Lear*. "Ah, Doctor Baird, you must remember to use the forceps next time," I suggest.

The patients in the waiting room look a little worried.

Saturday January 19
I am no longer waiting for the gift of sound and vision. The eye bandage comes off and I can see, though bright light is painful. After the surgery it's eye drops for five weeks and two weeks of sleeping with a protective plastic patch surgically taped over the eye (which is difficult to do in bed), and avoiding vigorous activity and water. As my vision returns colours look brighter and I notice that my wife's skin is white not yellow. The pointing on the brick wall through our kitchen window is suddenly distinct.

For a writer there's nothing worse than fear of losing your vision. I'm 59 and now my eyes are no longer short-sighted. It feels like being 18 again, but without the acne. No more remembering to take my lenses out after one pint too many. Unlike the Daleks, my vision is no longer impaired. I'm finally able to ditch my solutions and contact lens containers, gleefully dumping them in the recycling bin. The organic lenses in my eyes have gone, replaced by plastic, and there's no turning back — but this feels like a mini-miracle.

Monday January 21
Resting my eye from computer work today and watching a lot of *Doctor Who*, going through Series 1 with Christopher Eccleston. But I do send a pre-written idea to the *Guardian* about sharing the same surname as Theresa May and the endless puns it generates. Mayday, Mayhem, The Darling Buddies of May, Come What May... I think it's a good idea. But fearing they won't reply I also forward it on the *New Statesman* and *Metro*. If all three replied I would probably eat Theresa May's leopard print shoes.

Tuesday January 22

My redundancy money finally arrives from LCC, where, as an associate lecturer, I taught sports journalism for a few hours a week (plus lots of time marking essays) for 12 years. It's £2100, which is not a massive sum, but certainly helps my short-term difficulties; though £1000 has to immediately go to our insurance company, for the excess we have to pay before any subsidence repairs can be completed.

Friday January 25

The *Guardian* respond to my Theresa May idea, which is again a small victory. "I'm not sure it's quite right for G2 so I'm going to pass in this instance." But at least they acknowledge my existence.

Monday January 28

Two functioning eyes today and back to work. Send a review copy of *Man About Tarn* to *Cumbria Life* magazine as they have so far ignored it. Send an idea to the *Guardian* about the village council in Allendale banning the display Dalek that stands outside the Museum of Sci-Fi. It's a good story, which they ignore.

Shop at Lidl, then cook family dinner of courgette and feta lasagne for Nicola, Nell, Lola and her friend Oscar, the son of a TV director and museum curator. Lola and Oscar have set up a magazine at SOAS, *The Fight Continues,* which she brings us to view. I'm impressed, but also a little worried. "Be very careful you don't become a journalist," I warn her, only half-joking. She reminds me of my own excitement doing a fanzine back in the 1980s and then writing for Red Wedge, the loose collective of pop stars and arty types campaigning for a Labour government.

Nell retreats to the living room to revise for her mock A levels. I'm proud of my daughters. Soon Nell will have gone as well as Lola, and the house will be a lonelier place, just Nicola, myself and Vulcan, plus some paying guests.

Tuesday, January 29
Made two pence on AdSense. No KDP sales, but a book royalty payment for £41 comes in for *Goodbye to Boleyn* – though as it hasn't reached the £50 threshold I get nothing for six months (grind teeth). After my problems with jaw pain my wife has suggested visiting a life coach called Karen. It's a free taster session. We meet in a frosty Victoria Park in Hackney where Karen encourages her clients to walk among nature and open up.

She tells me to stop beating myself up for changes I have no control over. We stand beneath a tree. She traces a circle in the earth with a stick and asks me to stand inside. The circle represents me. Then she asks what I feel when people ask me what book I'm now working on. I reply that I feel embarrassment when I don't have a commission, that I am not a proper writer, that I should have an idea, that I might never have an idea again... She draws a semi-circle radiating outwards for each negative thought and soon they surround me. Her point is that I am projecting my own fears on to people asking an innocent question.

She takes me out of the circle and it's a relief to be clear of the waves of negativity. I end up feeling better about things. There might even be an article in this. It's been surprising how much I've talked and how quickly the session has gone. This would bore my family, but a life-coach has to listen.

Thursday January 31

One pence made on AdSense, one e-book sold on KDP today. But not a bad month with 14 print books and 14 e-books of *Man About Tarn* sold, netting £61.41 in royalties.

Nicola suggests renting out part of a room to a local green who wants to pay to store some filing cabinets and then come and work on their papers.

"One thing we do not need is more stuff," I mutter.

"You just lack imagination," she says.

"No, I lack space," I answer.

FEBRUARY

LITERARY FORGER — REACHING OUT — BAD TRACK — COMMISSION SHOCKER — WALKING CLASS HERO —A MAN OF SUBSIDENCE — UPLOADING ESSEX

Saturday February 2

Life coach Karen has told me to think creatively about my money worries. In the evening Nicola and myself go out to watch the film about Lee Israel, *Can You Ever Forgive Me?* It's less a movie and more of a career plan. Israel is patronised and ignored by her agent and is struggling to pay the rent. So she falls in with charming reprobate Richard E Grant, buys some antique typewriters and forges notes from the likes of Ernest Hemingway, Dorothy Parker and Noel Coward. There was a form of literary skill in it too, knowing just what sort of cutting comments writers would make about their rivals. Forging literary letters seems much more lucrative than writing. I wonder if there is a course in it somewhere?

Tuesday February 4
Discuss column ideas with Nicola while we are boiling the kettle for tea. "The *Guardian* wouldn't want someone like you, they'd get a young black bi girl," she suggests, not entirely helpfully. Should I perhaps repurpose my gender to maximise my chances of getting something published? I am a privileged white male, though it doesn't seem to be helping. Perhaps it is best to give up

on journalism entirely and concentrate on book ideas?

Could I be depressed, I wonder? Growing up in Essex it's not something I've ever thought about, most problems can be ameliorated with a quip. I wouldn't recognise depression if it turned up wearing a Joy Division overcoat and playing *So Long Marianne* by Leonard Cohen. But there have been niggling health ailments and now my wife has got me seeing a life coach. I've had 32 years of pitching freelance ideas, which inevitably means a lot of knock-backs as well as some successes.

Now the commissions aren't coming, the advances aren't arriving, the phone isn't ringing and I'm too old to be seen as a promising young writer. We thought the print industry would go on forever, that there would always be paid work. The disruptors have won and free content is everywhere on the internet. But it doesn't mean I won't stop trying. After all, when I first met Nicola at the *New Statesman* back in the 1990s the magazine was based in a building called Perseverance Works.

Tuesday February 5
Finish work early at 3.30pm to take the train up to Nell's sixth form parents evening in Finchley. The first appointment is set for 4.35. Nicola is teaching at LCC and Nell herself is in Brussels on a politics trip. So I join all the other parents queuing by desks and drinking tea in white plastic cups. Nell's teachers have only positive things to say about her and on the bus home I feel impressed by her self-motivation. I'm also armed with lots of information about student finance — and with my low income and Nicola's slightly higher but still slim receipts, she should certainly get a full loan.

Wednesday February 6
I have been busy promoting *Man About Tarn* on twitter,

following Lake District tweeters and doing a daily link to the book on Amazon. One of my tweets to likely Lakes lovers gets a sarky reply from a boot company; "Looking through your twitter feed you don't seem to RT anyone twitter works so much better when your (sic) social." This is followed by a thumbs-up emoji.

Please, spare me the patronising tone and the thumbs-up and the policing of my twitter feed. I'd been doing quite a lot of retweeting, though maybe not in recent days. It's tempting to do a Basil Fawlty and throw all the guests out of the twitter hotel. Do they know how hard it is to sell a book? To survive. Do they really think I can spend all day on twitter? Would Marcel Proust have spent all day retweeting? He might have struggled to describe *Remembrance of Things Past* in 280 characters.

Thursday February 7
Receive a rather Orwellian massage from Fiverr: "We've noticed that you haven't visited your Fiverr account recently. Staying active is important for the success of your business, and we'd like to make sure clients can find you. Just a heads up - your inactive Gigs will get automatically paused. Please reply to this email within the next 7 days to keep them active."

Meanwhile KDP's helpline thanks me for "reaching out" about the author copies of *Man About Tarn* that I can't seem to order. Author copies are only £2.55 each rather than the £7.99 full price, and so much better for selling to friends, only my order keeps failing to appear in my Amazon basket. It would be good to inform Amazon that I am not reaching out, it's more like exasperated and complaining. But eventually their help email does do the job and after deleting the cache and cookies on my old browser it seems to work again.

I start to write an imaginary *Doctor Who* episode

where Daleks reach out to humans and give a heads up that all inferior races will be automatically paused unless the Doctor surrenders within seven days.

Friday February 8

The agent who wrote in the Society of Authors' magazine *The Author* about not ignoring writers with "bad track" (a bad track record) because the failure of one book doesn't mean another won't succeed, emails back to say that she's not taking on any new clients. It seems I have more bad track than Southern Rail.

Years ago I thought agents would nurture me, provide advice, help with ideas, come to dinner parties. Back in 2005 I did have a couple of months with the agent of a well-known travel writer. After a few weeks she told me she wasn't getting anywhere with my ideas and dumped me. I felt very let down. Her other clients had radio shows she explained. "You'll say you've had longer one-night stands," she emailed. I wonder if in the #MeToo age I can claim for being treated badly in a metaphorical one-night stand with a literary agent?

In 2008 a much-better agent, David Luxton, got me a very reasonable £15k advance (minus his ten per cent) for my eco memoir *There's A Hippo In My Cistern* (the same book the previous agent gave up on). But there's no contract with an agent. *Hippo* sold 2700 copies, which is reasonable for a book with a minimal promotional budget, but not big money. It didn't result in lots of agents knocking at my door. David didn't go for any of my subsequent ideas, even though they were eventually published through my own negotiations with publishers. None of them made much in advances, so from a financial point of view he was probably right, though there was still tremendous satisfaction for me in seeing them reach an audience.

Agents want you to slap down a best-seller. And you can't really blame them, as they need writers with a big advance to get a decent cut. Today no-one wants midlist writers, even with 15 books to their name, not that I'm counting.

So for all my books bar *Hippo* I've relied on my own efforts to get a publishing deal. The advantage of this is that you don't have to pay a percentage to an agent; the disadvantage is that increasingly publishers only accept proposals from agents in what is a literary closed shop and an agent can normally negotiate a much bigger advance.

Saturday February 9
We celebrate Nell's 18th birthday with lunch at Gallipoli restaurant in Upper Street. My sister aka Auntie Kaz is there along with Granny Fiona and her partner Anthony. The waiters present a cake and do a dance to some Turkish music. Nell's birthday celebrations continue with a trip to see the Vaccines play with a group of her friends.

Monday February 11
Receive a Linkedin request to connect with a recruiter for writing a website. After some Googling I discover they offer just $5 a page. Send my Theresa May puns idea to the *Evening Standard*. Better news is that the editor of the *Author* magazine says that he is thinking about using an idea I sent him about the travails of a struggling writer and he will be getting back to me once he is commissioning.

A disturbed night in bed as Nell is out until one. She has been to Brick Lane and then disappears into a fractured space-time continuum of night buses and teenage gatherings. We receive various texts that she is "like ten minutes away" and "just leaving Jem's house".

Eventually she arrives and we can finally sleep soundly, knowing she has not been attacked by the phone thieves and crack dealers (probably ex-writers) who inhabit the streets near our house.

Tuesday February 12
Another hour with Karen the life coach, walking slowly around Victoria Park, only this time it's not a free taster session, I am paying her £75. Nicola says it is doing me good, if not my bank balance.

We do an exercise with Karen etching a circle in the dirt where I stand in the middle and radiating out are the semi-circles representing my feelings about my wife earning more (but not much more) than me. That I should be working harder, she is under too much pressure, I should be a patriarchal breadwinner, I am lazy, I am not doing enough, it is indulgent to be a writer.

It's quite rigorous intellectually, all this not analysing thoughts, but identifying what thoughts you are having. She picks me up on the words I use, when I say, "you tend to think it's your fault." "You need to use 'I' more, not 'you'…" says Karen. "And you say 'should' a lot, that puts pressure on yourself, you could try "I could do it' instead."

I tell her that attaching a CV to my emails helps and I think, "I'm not too bad". "This is too negative. You can say I am good! Without being arrogant," she admonishes. I wonder if I should be more positive like Joey from *Friends*, currently Nell's favourite viewing. "How *you* doin' Karen?"

Wednesday February 13
A sack of wood has appeared on our doorstep, another gift from the Wood Man. Only these bits are massive. He must imagine we have a chainsaw, whereas all we have is

a rusty hand saw in the cellar. He's left eight-foot long bits of decking and two six-foot long mysterious pieces of curved hardwood beam, which look as if they formed part of some mysterious Woodhenge-style temple where votive offerings were made to the tree divas.

Do a West Ham blog post. My cataract piece idea is rejected by the *Guardian*. It's expected, so shouldn't feel low, at least they answered. Keep going. Try elsewhere. Write list of possible ideas to try. Made 1p on AdSense. One e-book sold for £1.72. Should I increase my book price to get a bigger cut? Or reduce my Fiverr rates again? There must be ways to improve my cash flow.

Thursday February 14
Present Nicola with a home-made Valentine's Day card and a box of chocolates. Receive a Fiverr request from a man in the US asking if I am interested in writing sermons. I politely decline, as my knowledge of God doesn't extend much past watching *Rev*. Though I wonder if God is a good payer? Perhaps he/she will review some of my books on goodreads.com: "Being omnipotent, I read it in one sitting!"

Friday February 16
Nell has been on the schoolchildren's climate change protest at Westminster and is quoted in the *Times*. She's come out with a great soundbite: "I'm not here to miss school. If we don't do anything there won't be a school. I think group action in this sort of way always makes some sort of difference. Together we can make a difference." We talk about it over brunch. "It was easy, I just told the journalist what she wanted to hear," explains Nell. All those years of media training at her parents' hands have paid off.

Saturday February 17

Think up some titles for a Fiverr person in America who has written a self-published book on success. Strange how orders always seem to arrive at the weekend. But in the gig economy we are always available and in a couple of hours I've earned £9 commission.

Monday February 18

"Lord Sugar! Can you hear me Lord Sugar? I gave your *Apprentice* boys one hell of a beating!" I'm hired. The loneliness of the long-distance freelancer is over. I have a commission. Break out the victory bells. Since *Lakeland Walker* reviewed *Man About Tarn* I've established an e-mail rapport with John the editor, who also happens to be a *Doctor Who* fan. I'm being offered £175 for a piece on family walking. The editor is apologetic for the rates but his budget has been cut while I am ecstatic that someone wants to use my work. I must tell Karen my life-coach about this. Somebody is still using freelancers.

Tuesday February 19

Lola has stayed overnight in her old bedroom and is here for breakfast with Nell. The girls demand that I make them toasted Hippy Bread and coffee. Nell insists that I pour her water out because she can't move from the table. Who will pour her water when she is at university?

Email John at *Lakeland Walker* about my prospective feature. The latest subsidence survey arrives in my inbox showing 11mm of movement in our walls. Spend a lot of time trying to track down who edits Self & Wellbeing at the *Observer*. Which is not very good for my wellbeing. Then it's off to Moorfields for my post-op assessment. All seems to be good and there are no complications with my bionic eye.

Wednesday February 20

The door bell rings. "Would you like some fresh fish?" asks a man in a white coat. It's the fish sellers from South Shields who periodically tour affluent north London. At least they say they are from South Shields, they could just be cockney chancers who are good at sounding like Ant and Dec. "I'll just ask my wife," I suggest. He sells Nicola £10 of haddock. "It's fantastic fish, pet." Being an avid blogger she offers to interview him about his views on Islington. Nicola stores the fish in the freezer, along with several other pieces of frozen fish from their previous visits. She suggests, "It will be good brain food for Nell when she takes her A levels." Nell looks suspicious.

Monday February 25

The insurers' representatives arrive to take soil core samples from our front garden. The engineer deposits twenty round samples of London clay on top of the bike shed at the front of our house — they look rather like giant turds. Hopefully this is not some sort of metaphor for my career.

Deliver some Green Party leaflets (for free) on behalf of Nicola, who is a party member. It's a simple repetitive task, but I do get to see a lot of different front garden path designs and learn a lot more about letter-box design. Modern letter-boxes are difficult to open and have sections of brush inside that make poking leaflets through increasingly difficult. Could I do this for a living? It keeps me fit and there's a definite end product, which there isn't always in writing.

On a doorstep I meet local friends Diane and David. They ask what I'm working on and I use some of Karen's techniques saying "I don't have a big idea yet but I'm sure I will have one soon." They are encouraging and remind me that they have one of my books on their shelves at home. This makes me feel more positive.

Back home I start to write my piece on family walking for *Lakeland Walker*. It won't go in until the summer issue, but it's good to have a commission, to feel wanted, to be a walking-class hero.

Tuesday February 26

My 2012 book *The Joy of Essex* has gone out of print and last year the publishers returned some 300 books to me, as they no longer had room for them in their warehouse. They now sit in our attic and I sell them to friends and at any literary events I'm invited to. I've asked for the e-book rights back so that I can publish it myself on KDP. The paperwork has been completed and I've received a file of the full manuscript. I try to upload it to KDP, but it is the wrong sort of file. I have to try and get a Mobi-file, whatever that is. Then send my idea on the ignominy of being called May in the era of Theresa to the *Big Issue*.

Wed February 27

Sold 12 print copies and 12 e-books of *Man About Tarn* this month, plus one e-book of *Whovian Dad*. Receive £59.09 in royalties from KDP, plus $2.95 for a US sale.

Two pence made on AdSense today. Walk Vulcan after breakfast, then read *The Salt Path* by Raynor Winn, which is a great read even if I can't compete with Winn and her partner's problems.

A Mobi-file has arrived from the publisher and finally I republish *The Joy of Essex* on KDP. It doesn't sell a lot now, but if an e-copy is purchased then I get £1.72. Then redo the cover of another of my old books, *Sunday Muddy Sunday,* which I've now self-published on KDP after the rights from Virgin Publishing reverted to me when it went out of print.

Send out some emails asking a couple of friends for references to go with my application to be a Fellow with the Royal Society of Literature. I'm not that optimistic about succeeding, but it's a chance to help students, good money and steady employment. Perhaps for once they will want a literary geezer rather than an Oxbridge-style Fellow.

MARCH

KARMA CHAMELEON — EAR TODAY GONE TOMORROW — CAREER OPPORTUNITIES — I'VE GOT THE MUSIC IN ME — A FRIDGE TOO FAR — GHOST WRITING

Monday March 4

An astonishing day. Am I a karma chameleon? There's a commission from the Society of Authors in my inbox. James the editor of *The Author* likes my idea of a spoof 'Diary of a Writing Nobody'. Ben Bradman wants me to do a week and a half's work on a tie-in book written by the CEO of a wellness app. A Brighton University student wants to interview me about West Ham for his dissertation. An Amazon commissioning editor answers an email I wrote three months ago. Are people just feeling good today? Or trying to use up their budgets? Is it the sun? Pre-Brexit panic? I'll take it, whatever it is. I meet Nicola on the doorstep and shake her hand, introducing myself with "Pete May, successful journalist". I've not said that for a long time. She looks pleased.

Tuesday March 5
Daughter Lola comes round with her flatmate Oscar for Pancake Day. She has had a long Facebook argument with an ex-friend about "white saviours" and Comic Relief after the recent Stacey Dooley controversy, when Dooley was photographed with an African baby. It resulted in mutual unfriending. "Life's too short to get

involved in complicated online discussions that only lead to being ghosted. Leave that to us writers," I tell her. Though yesterday it seems that I was miraculously un-ghosted by at least a few people of influence.

Wednesday March 6
It's the annual reunion dinner of *FC* magazine at a pizza place near Kings Cross. Once we all wrote about Sunday league football. David at least has a proper job at the *Financial Times*. Peter is doing ideas, Tony C is semi-retired and doing freelance design, the other Tony P is covering non-league football at the weekends and teaching English in the week and I'm also freelance, while the absent David Conn, another old FC writer, went on to find glory at the *Guardian* and as a writer of football books like *Richer Than God*. It's a miracle we can pay the bill, but it's always good to get out and meet other writers. It's good to know that we are not alone.

Thursday March 7
My ears have become muffled. The nurse at the local surgery has recommended a week's dousing in olive oil and then having them syringed. Nicola has dutifully had to place a drop of olive oil into my ears with a dropper device this morning. No indignity surprises a freelance writer whose body is falling apart.

So now it feels like I am underwater and submerged in olive oil. Everything is muffled, my sense of balance is skewed. So much so that, while picking up canine excrement deposited by Vulcan, I drop my wallet on the Parkland Walk. Rather like Danny the Drug Dealer in *Withnail and I,* my motor has gone. Back at Finsbury Park bus station I suddenly realise, with a feeling of dread, that my wallet pocket is empty.

But I notice there's a voicemail on my phone. Luckily

an honest woman from Crouch Hill has found my wallet including my business card and rings me up to say she has picked it up on the pavement. I leave Vulcan back at home and take the bus up the hill to Crouch End to retrieve it. I meet Catherine on the corner of her street and receive back my wallet, feeling an idiot and giving her a tenner to buy a drink or breakfast with.

Back home I return to the muffled work world. An email asks me to join Amazon's influencer programme. For a moment I am flattered to be thought of as an influencer. I apply to the email link. "Sorry you do not have enough followers."

Nicola spots a job advert in *Islington Tribune*: "Do you enjoy working outdoors, helping people and have good communication skills?"

"Is it for a Park Ranger in the Lake District?" I ask.

"Actually it's for a traffic warden," she says. "You could give it a go."

"As a writer I do know about excuses and missed deadlines," I mutter.

My wife then recommends an article in the *Evening Standard* magazine on Lil Miuquela. Lil is a robot. Could I employ an avatar or robo-influencer to write for me I wonder?

Friday March 8

My ears still feel like they are submerged in an ocean of olive oil. Rather like Beethoven, I am having to delve into strange musical realms while completely deaf.

Spend half the day writing two sample music biographies. A couple of weeks ago my neighbour Nick alerted me to an advert from a contact of his asking for freelance music biography writers. It's for a bibliographic services outfit up north. The money is poor, £10 a go, but my employer Jen assures me they can be written in less than an hour. It seems fairly simple, full name, birthplace, date of birth, and a potted history of albums, singles and memorable moments.

The American country singer Maren Morris is quite interesting to research though the other biography is of the late Andre Previn, which takes an age to write.

Monday March 11
Finally a trip to the GP's surgery and an appointment with the nurse for a damn good ear-syringing. She tells me lots of risk factors but I go ahead, probably because I can't really hear her. The swishing starts, a sort of power shower of the ear. The relief is instant after she quickly unearths a bucketful of wax, plus a copy of Shakespeare and the Bible.

In the evening I play for the Beta Males in the pub quiz at the Faltering Fullback with my old mates Bob, Woody, Adrian, Andrew and guest quizzer Bob's mate Nate. Ears revived, I can hear the quizmaster. After a poor start we use all our experience to deduce that William Perry is nicknamed The Fridge, Malaga is Spain's sixth most populated city, Stanley Holloway is the comic singer famous for his monologues, and sensing that 'aga' might be a theme, agate emerges as the banded rock found in Sicily and we then identify the Aga Khan as the British-born current Imam of Nizari Isma'ilism.

The Beta Males actually win, fired up by beer, crisps, peanuts, pork scratchings and a love of trivia, banking the winner's prize of £50. It can only be a matter of time before we turn professional. Quizzing is quite probably better paid than writing, and comes with superior snacks.

Tuesday March 13
A cold call from the company that designed my website. On the other end of the phone is an aggressive salesman

with a northern accent wanting to redo my website in WordPress so it's mobile friendly, all for just £500. Seeing that I have already paid the company once to design it, I'm not paying them again. Once I tell him that print journalism is disappearing it seems to get rid of him.

Spend the rest of the day preparing my application to the Royal Society of Literature to be a Fellow. This is a three-day a week post where you discuss students' writing with them at a given university for two days a week for a tempting £15k — though this must be tempting many other writers too. Four years ago the RSL rejected my application and said I couldn't re-apply until I'd written another two books. Which I have now done. I've blagged two references from my journalist pal Nigel at the *i* newspaper and Mark, with whom I taught sports journalism at LCC.

Now I have to convince myself that I am pompous and I have literary merit, one of their key criteria. It's a good feeling to write down a list of my books, the anthologies I've written in, my journalism and sub-editing experience, plus "other literary experience" and "writing workshops, residencies held or other types of literary teaching experience". Ha, I've done an event at the Essex Literary Festival! And lots of events at the Newham Bookshop and East London libraries. I've delivered talks at the University of Brighton and University of Hertfordshire and chaired a *Doctor Who* talk at the Loughton Library — which is probably the greatest achievement of my life. My personal statement takes a lot of research into my back pages, though by the end of it I'm certainly prepared to employ myself.

Thursday March 14
Go to the launch of my pal Adrian Whittaker's book, *Dr Strangely Strange: Fitting Pieces to the Jigsaw*, at the

Stoke Newington Bookshop.

Dr Strangely Strange were an experimental Dublin folk group formed in 1967. The original band only made two albums, before reforming in the late 1990s. It's niche stuff, but Adrian has managed to get a review in the *Sun* of all places. He's done a great job tracking down the band and seeing what they remember of the Sixties. He's also the author of a previous book on the Incredible String Band.

As Adrian is a member of my pub quiz team, the Beta Males, we just have to hope that eventually a question will come up on Dr Strangely Strange so he can utilise his incredible mind palace that is stocked full of folk-rock trivia.

As Adrian delivers his speech I discover that *Heavy Petting*, Dr Strangely Strange's very rare acid folk LP is worth £600 and he has a copy. Songs such as *Ballad of the Wasps* sum up the vibe. It's a pleasant evening of wine among the bookshelves. Once publishers would pay for lavish book launches, but these days authors invariably have to organise any kind of launch themselves. But marking the achievement of completing a book is important for us writers and a glass of wine with friends makes the lonely hours in front of the keyboard all seem worthwhile.

Saturday March 16
Have made 21p on AdSense. Hannah from Wales comes to stay with us and immediately starts to scrub our kitchen table and remove the crumbs from the joins in the fold-down section. Is she trying to tell us something?

Tuesday March 19
Result. The ghost writing work has materialised courtesy of Ben Bradman. It's for a book going out under the

moniker of a person who founded a wellness app. Though the ghostwriter needs someone to do the bits she hasn't got time for. So I'm ghostwriting for a ghostwriter, which makes me positively spiritual. On the positive side I have been promised a credit in the book's acknowledgements and incredibly they are paying £200 a day. That's almost grown-up money and I will do any amount of third-hand ghosting for that much.

Thursday March 21
My final session with Karen the life-coach. She's asked me to write down a list of positive things that have happened to me. I've come up with Vulcan being pleased to see me when I get in from the pub as one example, though when I add that dogs don't judge you, she is quick to ask if I feel that people do judge me. My other positive things are sunlight on the brickwork seen through my kitchen window on a frosty morning; Lola says her friend Michael admires me as I have written books about *Doctor Who* and West Ham; the fact Nell's friend Beth's mum has read one of my old books; lighting the wood burner on a snowy night; the fact Nicola says I have been a good dad.

I'm also able to tell her that she might have bought some good karma as I've sold a couple of pieces from emails I wrote ages ago and got a two-week job ghost-writing. It would have been easy to give up. But looking at different avenues and not blaming myself might have worked. And if nothing else I've got to know Victoria Park and its fine old bandstand a lot better as we must have done numerous circuits of it. You can't succeed without failure and industries change. Perhaps I don't need to give myself such a hard time.

All this extra work is useful in another way, as wellness doesn't come cheap at £75 for each of these sessions. We walk around a chilly Victoria Park, our boots crunching on frosty grass as I reflect that really I'm paying someone to listen to me talk about relative failure. But it's helped. We have come to the end of our four-class session and she effectively discharges me. I feel like I have passed some kind of test.

Karen says a bad thought takes one tenth of the time to go into my head compared to a good thought because humans are hardwired to look for threats (and dodgy commissioning editors). She wants me to remember the techniques she has mentioned to concentrate on my breathing when I take breaks from work, to look at nature for at least 12 seconds at a time, to keep noting down positive things. Self-help therapy might feel like I'm in an episode of *Fleabag*, but as an isolated freelancer it has helped to talk to someone other than my desktop.

Monday March 25
The fridge is humming loudly and making ominous rumbling noises. A green light is flashing on its front and the freezer is starting to smell of South Shields haddock. Nicola and myself spend the morning trying to repair it by removing ice from around the fan. This involves sliding the fridge-freezer out of its fitted kitchen unit. As preparation we spend the morning removing numerous jars of pickles from it, mainly given to us as gifts by visitors from Wales where they love their preserves, all kept by Nicola just in case we might need them. Then we pull the weighty fridge freezer out from its unit.

We place the malfunctioning fridge on a platform constructed from of pieces of wood that arrived on our doorstep from the Wood Man. We knew his wood deposits might eventually be useful for something. There's a huge pile of dirt under it and behind lies a thick layer of dust plus an ancient hummus container and mini-marmalade jar. We try to remove the ice and then give up and call an engineer. He melts the ice with what appears to be a giant hairdryer. Later we discover it makes no difference to the performance of our dodgy appliance. Clearly we have travelled a fridge too far.

In the afternoon I am allowed to return to writing. For once I have too much work. Five music biographies have come in. The trick is to try and do each artist or band in one hour and not spend forever trying to find the date of birth of a J-pop singer if it's not easily available. Researching the French singer Etienne Dohl impresses my elder daughter Lola who spent her gap year in Paris and likes the demi-monde world of louche Parisian singers. Then I work on ghostwriting methods of getting a good night's sleep for the wellness app book.

Wednesday March 27
The fridge is still making asthmatic noises like Darth Vader More work on the wellness app book. A clicker in Canada has made me £1.21 on AdSense. Must be the mature singles ads. While Theresa May's government seems paralysed by Brexit, I have completed a deal or two myself this month.

Nicola and myself debate who is going to call the fridge company again and be put on hold for aeons listening to tinny Mozart.

"I bet David Cameron doesn't have to ring up Zanussi now he's retired to his shepherd's hut!" exclaims Nicola.

"And nor did he have to sweep the extension or wash up because the lodgers are here," I add.

Eventually Nicola gets through and the engineer is coming tomorrow after a cancelled appointment.

I cook sausages, soft carrots and my special mashed potato for dinner to compensate Nell for the fridge debacle. Nicola is busy organising an exhibition of photos from her Islington Faces blog to be shown at Islington Museum. She says her photographer pal Kimi won't be there for the hangings, as she can't get time off from her day job. "Isn't capital punishment a bit extreme for your subjects?" I venture.

Thursday March 28
A look at today's papers reveals lots of headlines apparently about me, such as, "Give May Just a Little More Time" and "The End of May". The Commons is in chaos as MPs reject Theresa May's Brexit deal and she's going to quit on May 22.

The engineer arrives and says that in the long-term we might need a new fridge. The current one needs new dilithium crystals or something like that and no amount of de-icing the fan will save it. Still, we might be able to limp on with it for a bit longer. We're not sure how much a new fridge/freezer will cost, but it will be a lot.

Write my music biographies and then a section on dream-themed films for the wellness app book. Nicola arrives home frazzled after teaching her uni students all morning and has to go for a bike ride to get some physical stimulus

Young Nell is revising for her mock A levels and announces at dinner that she is worried that her friends are more worried about their A levels than she is. We tell her that calmness is a good thing. I add that I didn't get where I am today by going from wimp to worrier.

Friday March 29
Man About Tarn was published a year ago today. I mark this with a post on my Facebook page: "Thanks to all have helped with the success of *Man About Tarn*, including *Lakeland Walker, Cumbria* and *Country Walking* magazines for some great reviews, the

Romanticism blog for reproducing my chapter on Wordsworth and the Campaign for National Parks for hosting my blog on the book. Most of all, thanks to all the readers who have put up positive reviews on Amazon. If it's impressed a few people in walking socks then it's all been worthwhile."

Sold nine print copies and four e-books of *Man About Tarn* this month, plus two e-books of *The Joy of Essex* and one print version of *Flying So High*. Receive £34.63 in royalties from KDP plus $0.06 for a few pages read on Kindle Unlimited in the US.

Finish my ghostwriting for the wellness app. That's seven days at £200 per day making £1400. That's equivalent to what I earned in six months last year. The company is based in the USA and promises to pay promptly and efficiently, in British pounds. My own wellness feels considerably enhanced.

Then finish off the week's music biographies. For the first time in ages I am fully employed. Email off my invoices with a feeling of triumph. A lecturer from Herts University rings asking me about what might be taught on a sports journalism MA course. I offer to send her a quick outline, but hope she's not asking me if I'm interested.

Do I want to go back to standing in front of a class with imposter syndrome while students demand to know why they are paying 9K in fees? Hopefully I've helped some students in my time. But I've given 12 years to part-time teaching. Writing is what I want to do, even if it means more hack work and just about surviving.

APRIL

FOR FOX SAKE — REVOLVING EDITORS — THE WHOLE TOOTH — BOOKS AS INSULATION — MY LOST MASTERPIECE — SILLY MUGGERS

Monday April 1

My sprits sink a little at receiving the names of four rappers and one jazz musician to write brief biographies on. Do I really want to be doing this? Still it's weekly money, that's something.

My friend Nigel has sent over a reference for my application to be a Royal Society of Literature Fellow. When in doubt use your West Ham-supporting mates. And he's good enough to say some nice things about me.

I post off the voluminous application form, feeling rather pleased that I've had to add a separate list of my many publications, as the space on the form isn't big enough. I decide not to include the *ALCS News* piece on my portfolio career income though, where I reveal that I could earn more working at an Amazon warehouse than writing books, as it might make me look too much like an underachiever.

Nicola gives me several envelopes of her *Pavement* magazine to take to the Post Office and post to various homeless charities as it will help her out and she's on deadline.

Tuesday April 2
Morning has broken. As I let the chickens out of their

inner coop and into their run, Vulcan discovers a white plastic bag of takeaway food left by the fox, which has been dining *al fresco* in our garden overnight. I pick up the shredded plastic bag, several pieces of polystyrene burger container complete with tooth marks and tomato ketchup on them, a plastic fork and several tissues. Throwing them in the dustbin I wash my hands carefully, mindful of fox-borne diseases.

Vulcan then spots Joe the cat from next door over the garden wall and barks at maximum volume. The cat looks unmoved. Wolfie, the giant dog in the garden two doors down starts to bark too, in great gruff *Hound of the Baskervilles* bellows. My mornings are rarely mindful.

Our friend Christian comes down from Bangor to stay. He is attending a meeting of Friends of the Earth. Christian is a Whovian and has bought down a copy of *The Macra Terror*, an animated version of the old Patrick Troughton-era *Doctor Who* story. The original footage was wiped by the BBC in the 1960s. Christian and myself can't resist watching a couple of episodes and the animation is surprisingly good, alongside the original audio recording. Though it is a distraction for a man trying to work from home.

Wednesday April 3
A fox is sitting on the roof of the chicken coop with a burger container as I let Vulcan out in the morning. There's an uneasy stand-off as I grab Vulcan and lunge at the fox with a mop. It looks a little indignant and gently jumps over the back fence and into the street, while Vulcan and myself stand in the corner of the garden growling, ready to repel all invaders.

Watch the final two episodes of *The Macra Terror* (it's good, particularly as I haven't seen it since I was eight-years-old) before getting down to writing some music biographies. Interrupted by Nicola wanting me to change the light bulb in bathroom. How many writers does it take to change a light bulb? One, who can't afford to rent an office. One of the problems of being freelance is how domestic tasks infringe upon the working day. Or they get ignored. Meanwhile the fridge is still on life support.

The AdSense revenue for my blogs has gone up to £47 with the latest monthly figures, slowly getting towards the £60 threshold. A deposit of £70 arrives in my bank account for the first batch of music biographies. It's always a relief when a new client proves to actually have money to pay you with and does so promptly.

Thursday April 4
Churn out more biographies. In the evening it's Nicola's Islington Faces exhibition at Islington Museum. It features photographer Kimi Gill's great pictures of ordinary Islington folk interviewed for Islington Faces by Nicola.

She's put huge effort into the blog, interviewing one person a week even though she isn't paid for her labour. But it's paid off in goodwill and the characters she's met. The Mayor of Islington is at the Museum launch along with subjects like London's happiest bus driver, uber Arsenal fan Mick, the council receptionist who is a former international basketball player and a woman who makes necklaces out of clay pipes found on the Thames foreshore. There's even a free glass of wine and some crisps. Well done Nicola. She is a woman of substance, even if we live in a house of subsidence.

Friday April 5
A book has sold on KDP. One pence income on AdSense. Write a West Ham blog post; finish off my final music

biography of the week. Another of my editors has moved on. Andrew who commissioned *Man About Tarn* for Amazon's Kindle Single series has now moved on to Amazon Audible and the Kindle Single series is being discontinued, as e-books haven't killed off paperbacks as everyone once assumed they would.

The publishing world seems bizarrely fluid. When I started out I assumed a writer would establish a long-lasting relationship with one editor. Ben who published *Sunday Muddy Sunday* at Virgin Books rapidly moved on. Claire who commissioned *There's a Hippo In My Cistern* at HarperCollins was almost immediately made redundant and ended up working for a publisher in Australia. Bill who commissioned my Mainstream books *Rent Boy, Irons in the Soul* and *Hammers in the Heart* retired and then Mainstream was sold to Random House. Iain Dale who commissioned my books *The Joy of Essex* and *Goodbye to Boleyn* has moved on to work for LBC and become a full-time political pundit. Any editors who publish me should be careful; they will inevitably be moving on before they can publish my next midlist non-blockbuster.

Monday April 8

Very pleasingly £1200 arrives in my bank account, the payment for my work on the wellness app. But now I'm also in acute pain from a dodgy gum. On Saturday Nicola and myself went to Andrew and Trista's party in the house next door. They are both financial journalists and as they write about something useful like money they still earn a living. But drinking a can of Punk IPA I started to note that my gum hurt and it felt like maybe an abscess. It felt worse yesterday. Today I have an emergency appointment at my dentist. He prods about in my mouth and discovers that there is a loose flap of skin on my gum with a tooth beneath it. This might be something to do with my tooth grinding; now I have ground away part of my gum. It really hurts when the skin-flap gets moved. On Wednesday the dentist wants me to return where he will cut away the excess gum and expose the tooth beneath.

Tuesday April 9
My West Ham blog post has made 1p on AdSense. I'm hurting as I check the stats. Footballers play through the pain barrier — I'm writing through the tooth barrier. My mouth feels poisoned but there are seven music biographies to complete this week. I'm trying to write a biography of Marco Mengoni, who is not a footballer but an Italian pop star.

Some good news is that to mark Wordsworth's birthday the Wordsworth Trust has retweeted my *Man About Tarn* chapter on Wordsworth and his Lake District homes. They had originally reproduced it in their Romanticism Blog last year soon after the book came out and are now giving the piece another plug. As the blog has 32,000 followers it's very useful publicity. Though I'm not sure what Wordsworth would have made of twitter; he'd have probably had Dorothy running his social media accounts, tweeting images of daffodils while he lay on his couch.

Wed April 10
Go to the dentist and have part of my gum removed. Basically the dentist scrapes around with what seems to be a Stanley knife and fully exposes a tooth that has been lying under my gum my whole life. It seems quite a result to get a new tooth at 59, although the pain is much worse than I had imagined. It feels like I'm Dustin Hoffman in *Marathon Man*. I'm knocked out and return home to bed.

In the evening Nicola's pal Nicky and some other friends come over to dinner. I can hear them all talking downstairs. Nicky insists on coming upstairs to see me in my dimly-lit bedroom, dosed up on painkillers. Perhaps she doubts if it's really me, rather like in *Fawlty Towers* when, at the insistence of Basil, Polly has to lie in bed pretending to be an ill Sybil.

Thursday April 11
Take some painkillers and sit at my computer to complete the final two music biographies for the week. Not sure if it's worth it at £10 a go but a good hack always meets his deadlines.

Friday April 12
My gum is a little less painful. Go up to the attic to fetch some more copies of *There's a Hippo In My Cistern* and *The Joy of Essex* for a forthcoming writers' stall. I open the hatch in the landing ceiling, pull down the extendable ladder and clamber up the steel rungs. The attic contains the combined clobber of two writers and journalists. I crawl past my boxes of West Ham programmes, old copies of *Midweek* magazine, some early editions of *Loaded* from the 1990s, my old Amstrad computer, a box of VHS videos and a box of Nicola's letters, once contained in a black bin liner that is now disintegrating into flakes of black plastic.

Here lie several large industry-sized sealed plastic pallets of my books. Approximately 300 copies of *The Joy of Essex* and 250 *There's a Hippo In My Cisterns* were returned to me when they eventually went out of print. Publishers don't tend to keep your book in print beyond a few years unless it's a bestseller. Eventually they want to free up warehouse space and offer the books back to the writer. The alternative is for them to be pulped, which seems like sacrilege. They have been useful for selling at Christmas to friends, as parting gifts for our lodgers and at my writers' book stalls at the local Ecology Centre. But there are still an awful lot left. Though the boxes of books across the wooden boards of the attic also have another use, as they make great loft insulation. My words are literally keeping me warm.

Saturday April 13, Sunday April 14
Nicola has gone to Lulworth Cove for a bonding session with daughter Lola and Lola's godmother Hannah. So spend a quiet weekend recovering from gum pain and walking the dog.

Monday April 15
Why is there always firefighting? I have been trying to 'pair up' my e-books and paperbacks on Amazon so they both appear in the same listing. While doing this I discover that there is no e-book of one of my old books, *Flying So High: West Ham's Cup Finals*. Which is mystifying as the publishers changed hands a year ago and I spent a long time reformatting the book with a good editor. It was then republished a year ago, except it's not online now. So that's a year's sales lost, not that they would have amounted to much. But it's the principle of it.

I fire off a rude email and demand compensation. Then write to the Society of Authors for some legal advice and demand the rights back from my publisher. The clue is surely in the name *publisher*. If they don't actually publish then what is their function? My teeth can't take this. Perhaps my publishers also hijacked Flight MH370 and lost it somewhere online.

Tuesday April 16
Eventually I track down the former editor who a year ago

seemed easy to deal with and said it was all up and online. She is now doing a creative writing course at university. She is very apologetic and says it was published, but she thinks her old company must have messed it up when they changed to a new system. It's more cock-up than conspiracy. The publisher agrees to return the rights to me with unusual alacrity and I look forward to re-publishing it again on KDP. At least, like the Brexiteers, I have taken back control of my back catalogue.

Send an idea to the *Observer* magazine's Self & Wellbeing section about my sessions with Karen. Read some old copies of the Family section of the *Guardian* to try and think up some ideas for features.

Wednesday April 17
Another sack of wood has appeared on our doorstep from the phantom Wood Man. He's clearly been doing a lot of stuff with decking, though his offcuts of smaller wood might come in handy. The problem is we won't be lighting the log burner until the autumn and we've also been collecting bags of privet hedge sticks as kindling. Our cellar is now a giant tinder box ready to consume most of N4.

Back to my £10 a go musical biographies. I'd imagined some exciting rock stars, but the biographical library employing me want entries of various semi-obscure acts from all around the world. There's a *Schlager* singer who appears to be a German version of Chas and Dave, a middle-class French rapper, a Norwegian electronic duo, a Danish rock legend (in Denmark at least) and an Italian winner of *X-Factor*. Oh well, it's money.

When our Yorkshire friend Fleur last came to stay she asked, with that Yorkshire air of practicality, "Why doesn't Pete get a part-time job in an off licence?" At least this is keeping me away from the bargain wine bins, selling Stella and Doritos.

Thursday April 18
An e-mail from Fiverr: "Since we haven't heard back from you, we assume you are currently unavailable to work on Fiverr. Your Gigs have been paused and removed from our listings. You can always jump back in and reactivate them." I decide to jump back out now I have the music biographies as more regular low-paid work.

Friday April 19
We discover that Nell has been sort-of-mugged the previous evening. She has been leading the increasingly erratic hours of the upper sixth-former, arriving home in the small hours after evenings at 'Jem's house', a boy with a very patient or very long-suffering father who doesn't mind teenage gatherings at all hours. This incident happened at the relatively early hour of ten pm. While she was walking with a male friend across Highbury Fields a group of youths on bikes surrounded them and took her friend's iPhone.

They seem to have been inexperienced muggers though as they then engaged in a long and sexist debate about whether it was ok to also steal Nell's phone. "It would be really peak to take a girl's phone!" Nell tells them with all the street wisdom of a state-school educated north Londoner. And bizarrely they agree, cycling off, leaving Nell with her phone. It's worrying, but we manage to laugh about it too. "Have you ever been mugged Dad?" asks Nell. "Only by the publishing industry!" I reply, thinking of my royalties.

Monday April 22
Read *Extreme Sleeps* by Phoebe Smith, a book about sleeping in odd places like the shelter stone in the Cairngorms and a wrecked aircraft in Derbyshire. Could I write a book on extreme something? Extreme dog walking perhaps? Should I even be working on a bank holiday? Reading seems a compromise, and then I update my diary. A good writer always keeps a record of their life for future use.

Tuesday April 23
Our fridge is now giving out completely. Nicola announces that she has to cook everything in the defrosting freezer in order not to waste it. Lola is over from Turnpike Lane for our family dinner accompanied by an old sixth form friend. Her sister Nell looks distraught at the various dishes we are served. These are what Nicola has been saving to get us through the coming green apocalypse. There's mashed potato with olive paste, and slightly-off tofu with broccoli and mulled wine. Then a choice of fish or pasta, and an unspecified dish of mixed-up remnants. "That looks like sick!" says Nell, not entirely helpfully.

Wednesday April 24
Nicola rings up a well-known department store to order a new fridge which is going to cost a huge amount and take a couple of weeks to deliver, as they also have to dispose of our old fridge. Our near-neighbour Caroline calls round to collect the free delicious dog food that Nicola has been sent by a PR to plug on her blog — Vulcan can't eat it because he has pancreatitis. Another neighbour Will drops round a cool box, which is put in my office area to store our perishables in. Our now empty fridge is making a loud rumbling noise, though the freezer is still semi-

working, if possibly a health risk.

But there's a boost on KDP. Probably through my chapter on Wordsworth being retweeted by the Wordsworth Trust, *Man About Tarn* has sold four Kindle copies in a day. This is enough to briefly propel it in to the top ten of Kindle UK Travel Books. It's still way down the list of general travel sales, but as part of the job of a writer is to project an image of success, I take a screen grab of the chart, which shows *Man About Tarn* at number seven sitting above two Bill Bryson books, *Notes from a Small Island* and *Icons of England.* It's also above *The Lonely Planet Guide to Scotland* and *Watling Street* by John Higgs. The image is dutifully shared on Facebook and twitter.

Readers tend to assume that if you get a book into any sort of top ten then you are a best-seller making piles of cash. In reality it's probably £8 worth of sales that has propelled my book up to the top ten, as e-books don't sell anything like paperbacks. But still I'll take the glory and the chance to look successful.

Thursday April 25
My wife and daughter suggest that I should write a novel. Or turn my memoirs into novels. But what do I feel passionate about? That will last 80,000 words? Do I need to go on a creative writing course? Plots have always been a problem and any novel of mine would be thinly-disguised autobiography. They say get a genre. Perhaps a crime series where a number of commissioning editors who turn down ideas from ageing hacks go missing...

Friday April 26
The last of the week's seven biographies is completed on a Finnish pop duo. I need a holiday. Help Ben Bradman with some PR phrases for a health product. Start to pack

for five days in the Lake District. Send out an invoice for the biographies. Nicola insists we eat more fish from the ailing freezer. It's clear she couldn't say no to the doorstep sellers from South Shields. We retreat to the Tate to see the Bonnard exhibition as a Friday night artistic treat.

Saturday April 27
Sold 11 print copies and 12 e-books of *Man About Tarn* this month. Receive £51.60 in royalties from KDP. Watch West Ham (incredibly) win at Spurs in the World's End with my pals Matt and Lisa. Then it's on to see Nicola's exhibition at Islington Museum where we meet several of the old parents from our daughters' old primary school and have a drink in a pub called — in not very woke fashion — The Peasant. Presumably it's named after a freelance writer.

MAY

SUMMIT FOR THE WEEKEND — AGAINST ALL TERRIERS — HAMMERS IN THE HEART — THE WORLD'S WORST PADDLEBOARDER — THE ICE MAN COMETH — SETTING OUT MY STALL — NOT A FELLOW JUST A BLOKE — RAT ATTACK — TRUMP FLIES IN

Monday April 29-Friday May 3

Freedom arrives with a morning train to Penrith. Going to the Lake District for four nights always helps replenish this knackered freelancer. In a way it's also work. My last book *Man About Tarn* is still selling reasonably. I have 85 Wainwright fells left to complete and if I write up each trip as a chapter, a book might soon write itself.

It's unusually hot and sunny at Glenridding as I head to the youth hostel and the luxury of a four-bunk room to myself for a bargain £26 a night. The next day it's a huge 18-mile yomp, up Sticks Pass to complete the new fells of Hart Side and then Clough Head, via Stybarrow Dodd, Great Dodd and Watson's Dodd, making me feel like the Dodd man out. The second day is lost to tired muscles and a failed attempt to scale The Nab, but on subsequent days I also manage to bag Wether Hill via a lovely ferry ride across Ullswater to How Town and on my final day Hartsop above How.

Feeling small up against the mountains does me good.

Problems feel insignificant here as descending from
Hartsop above-How, a Maytree is in full blossom against
the dramatic backdrop of St Sunday Crag. No music
biographies this week, no scrutinising of sales figures, no
pitching of ideas. I return to London on a Friday evening
in muddy trousers, drinking a bottle of Hawkshead Red
feeling somewhat replenished.

Tuesday May 7
"You look like a vampire there's blood on your lip!" says
Nicola. My 18-mile walk in the Lake District pushed my
body too far and a cold sore emerged on my lip. The scab
has just burst with Dracula-like effect.

Back home but there is still no fridge. While many of
my friends are at the peak of their careers, a fridge will
severely stretch my resources. I will have to transfer more
of my diminishing capital (and my children's inheritance)
into my current account to cope.

However, one bonus of being fridge-less is that I have
just spooned ten-years' worth of jars of chutney and
pickles into the recycling bin. Nicola insisted on keeping
them as you never know when they might be needed.

We have a system to cope without a fridge now. We
buy as much as we can on the day of use and the cool box
that neighbours Will and Steve lent us is now on the floor
by my desk and is used to store wine, cans of Punk IPA,
oat milk, jars of pesto and pieces of yellowing organic
spinach. My writing area is in the extension on the cooler
north side of the house, so now it houses bottles of just-
about-not-curdling milk on the shelves along with
Nicola's ransom pesto and a saucepan of raggu. On no
account am I to turn on the portable heater, says Nicola,
even though it's quite cold for May.

My workspace is now less an office and more a walk-
in pantry. While in the garden a black bucket full of

water is home to Nicola's white wine, which she buys in refillable bottles from Borough Wines in Stoke Newington. Inadvertently we seem to have gone off-grid.

Wednesday May 8
Disaster! We have ordered the wrong fridge. Nicola has discovered that an inexperienced department store operative has directed her towards a fridge that has no door, designed for an integrated door in a modern kitchen unit. We have to start the ordering process again and it's going to take a week or longer to arrive, although this model is only £300 instead of nearly £600. I feel a little like Ernest Shackleton experiencing ever-new perils at each turn. Only at least he had access to ice.

Back to doing some music biographies. This week it's two drill rappers, French rock and rollers Les Chats Sauvages, Scandinavian house act Tungevaag & Rabaan and soundtrack writer Benjamin Wallfisch. Watching drill rappers gets a little tedious as what I don't need is young men waving wads of £20 notes at me as young women gyrate their posteriors. I thought all this hyper-macho posturing went out with the arrival of punk back in 1977. Perhaps it is all performance reflecting on bleak lives of gangland despair. Maybe it's designed to wind up old gits like me, but it's all a little depressing and childish.

Thursday May 9
Send off my West Ham answers to the *Observer* for their fans' round-up. It's unpaid, but gets my name in the paper at least.

Fleur from Yorkshire arrives. She is a long-standing friend of Nicola and a rather tweedy outcast in London circles.

"Why do you have a sign saying 'Against all terriers' on your door?" she asks.

Nicola chuckles. Overhearing this, I say, "Yes, we hate them all, apart from Vulcan,"

It seems Fleur has misread our poster, put up after the Finsbury Park mosque attack, reading, "Against all terror."

We get out the instant coffee for her, which she prefers to ground beans, enough to have us drummed out of Islington if word ever gets out. We also have to hope that no-one discovers that Fleur is down to do something with Conservative women. "Isn't Brexit going well?" I quip. No doubt she will be returning to north Yorkshire with tales of how in Corbyn's Islington they can't even afford fridges.

Saturday May 11
Nicola has talked me into going on a paddleboarding tour of the Regent's Canal at Angel, stopping by the towpath to listen to experts detail the architectural features of the canal side buildings. It's one of the tie-in events attached to her Islington Faces exhibition, but is suffering from a low turn-out. So photographer Kimi and myself are reluctantly placed on paddleboards, attached to our legs by a Velcro-strap. Standing up is very wobbly. I can only kneel and it's murder on my calves. My core is non-existent and my legs have the flexibility of oak. It's difficult to concentrate on the speakers Nicola has laid on. Perhaps I'm not a natural paddleboarder.

Sunday May 12
A satisfying day today running a local writers book stall at the Islington Ecology centre's spring celebration. As there are more writers per square foot than in any other borough in the world it's fairly easy to acquire some local tomes and wheel them in Nicola's warrior trolley to the Ecology Centre. Our near neighbour Katherine's

children's books sell particularly well and Nick and Nicolette (the Margot and Jerry to our Tom and Barbara) have provided copies of their tomes *The Plimsoll Sensation* and *Don't Sweat the Aubergine.*

It feels good to sell a physical product, to meet the people who might actually read something I've written. Nicola sells a *Save Cash and Save The Planet,* while I sell one *Whovian Dad,* one *Man About Tarn* and one *There's a Hippo In My Cistern.* Jeremy Corbyn makes an appearance but says he isn't allowed to buy any more books. I'm £20 richer at the end of the day and for once I feel successful and valued — putting a book in someone's hand is so much better than seeing a statistic on a royalty statement.

Monday May 13
Finally the fridge arrives in the late afternoon. They even take our old fridge away for recycling. Removing all the fridge magnets and alphabet letters from the front of it evokes a flood of Proustian memories of raising children.

We're not allowed to turn the new fridge on for five hours as the gas has to settle, but we sit and admire it, anticipating cold alcohol and being able to buy more than one day's provisions at a time from Lidl. It's gleaming white and has none of the stains and shattered plastic of our old knackered Zanussi.

"How is the fridge?" asks daughter Lola on WhatsApp.

"It's chillin' at the moment," I reply.

"Does this mean we can have proper food?" asks Nell.

With some satisfaction I remove two bottles of milk and a packet of spinach from my office and in to the new fridge. At 11pm we finally turn it on.

Tuesday May 14

Based on my forthcoming piece for the *Author* on the 'Diary of a Writing Nobody' I send a book proposal to Victoria at the print wing of Amazon. Start writing up a 3000-word account of my recent Lake District trip. What I really need is an advance to finance my travels. I remember advances, they were big in the Seventies. Go to see a play about Nell Gwynne at the Hen and Chickens theatre with Nicola and our Nell (no relation).

Thursday May 16
"Why is there a rat down the toilet?" asks Nell at breakfast.
I rush upstairs, thinking she can't be right. But no, inside the bowl is a drenched rat, struggling to climb up the porcelain. Nell seems to have taken it remarkably calmly, as if such occurrences are normal in our house. Perhaps they are.
"Jesus Christ, oh my God, we'll put the lid down and not panic," I tell her, panicking. "Nicola! There's a rat down the loo!"
Nicola comes up stairs to assess the situation. "I'm going to need a container, some gloves and a tea towel," she says.
"The window's open it might have got in that way. Or it might have swum up the U-bend…." I surmise.
"We're right behind you Nicola," I say, cowering behind Nell on the landing as Nicola puts her gloves on with the air of a seasoned rat catcher. She lifts the lid of the loo and expertly places a tea towel over the struggling rat. Then she places her gloved hands around the rodent and deposits it in a Quality Street tin, closing the lid.
"Well done! What do we do now?"
"We can release it in the park."
"What if it's a homing rat?"

"Well, we've got to put it somewhere. Nell, you'd better get off to college."

We start to walk down our road carrying the Quality Street tin. Only we bump into Stephen our local vicar. Nicola starts to chat to him. I pray the satanic rat doesn't start pounding on the tin. Or leap out and attack him. "Erm, we've got to get going to that appointment, Nicola," I mutter envisaging the *Islington Tribune* headline of, "Local Vicar Savaged by Rat-Wielding Devil Worshippers."

Once we've made it up the hill in Finsbury Park we approach the fence by the railway. "Look, if we just open it with the tin up against the fence it should run down the embankment."

We enact our plan, and the confused and bedraggled rat scarpers down the grass towards the railway. I start to hum the tune of *Born Free*. We've now done our bit for rat liberation.

Monday May 20
Complete my first two music biographies of the week, the first on American country singer Louise Ell, who isn't bad at all when I listen to her on YouTube. At least I am using some journalistic skills, getting key facts and condensing them into a brief career history.

Most musicians are like writers, affected by some piece of luck or key event that changes their career. I write another précis of the funk singer Betty Davis, who was singing forcefully about sex way before Madonna in the 1970s. Sadly she was largely ignored and gave up, before being re-appreciated in the new millennium. Thin lines between success and failure…

Then instead or writing more, I take our Black and Decker hedge-cutter and set to work on the mammoth privet hedge that stretches around the front garden of our corner house. It's tough work, stretching to cut the sharp twigs and leaves. Clouds of dust, pollen and pollution drift into my hair, up my nose and into my lungs.

"Nicola said I should get a hedge fund," I say to a neighbour who is picking his way over the mounds of cut leaves and branches. He looks blank. Sometimes my humour is wasted on real-life hedge fund managers.

Tuesday May 21
My usual morning tasks. Make coffee for Nicola in bed. Feed the dog and chickens. Nell is nervous as it is her first A level today. Her toast is too thick and the coffee is not warm enough. Nell tells her mum not to keep asking stupid questions. At least we get her off on the bus to college on time. A man comes to fix the sash window in Nicolas's office. She conducts an on-the spot interview with him about working-glass life.

In the afternoon Nicola and myself go on a guided *Diary of a Nobody* walk around the streets of Holloway. Our guide Jane shows us a number of houses that might match the original illustrations, and one by the railway line is a likely candidate to have been the fictional home where Charles Pooter lived. We learn about the new breed of Victorian commuters that was being satirised, the big stores and the trams that ran up and down the Holloway Road. Charles was a man struggling with middle-class life, dealing with endless callers at the door, annoying his wife with botched DIY and often making bad puns. Which sounds rather familiar.

Back in N4 Finsbury Park station is closed because of a suspicious vehicle, which proves to be a false alarm. Nell returns after her first A level, having been to McDonalds. This is a good sign. She says it didn't go too badly.

Thursday May 23
"Turning my compost did it, the worms are working much harder," says Nicola standing by our garden compost bin, before heading off in her jodhpurs and carrying a whip, ready to teach riding at Trent Park. An unusual get-up for the tube to Oakwood.

British Steel is closing, thus rendering redundant the line in XTC's *Making Plans For Nigel* about Nigel having his future in British Steel. Fire off an idea to the *Guardian's* Short Cuts section, which is rejected in seven minutes. Is it good they responded so quickly or bad they said no?

Friday May 24
It seems I am destined not to be a Fellow. A rejection letter arrives from the Royal Society of Literature. They will not be able to take my application further. They have received almost three times as many applications as they need. Competition has been extremely high. Trustees asked to convey their appreciation, etc. They rejected me four years ago and said I could only re-apply when I had written another two books. So I wrote two more and got my total up to 15. So now if I ever re-apply I will have to write another two and get it up to 17 and that might still not be good enough. An interview after 15 books and 12 years of teaching would have been something, even if I didn't get the job.

I start to imagine what life-coach Karen would make of it. She would have me holding a stick and drawing semi-circles in the soil representing my fears. That Thomas Paine was right and titles are but nicknames. That really you shouldn't have to write two extra books simply for the privilege of re-applying. That not giving any feedback means it seems like a closed shop. That perhaps there's an inflated idea of literary merit that doesn't cover football books. That it's ok for intellectuals to write about sex but not sport. Or is my rejection because I am a privileged white male? Or just not very good. And I'd have to let go of these fears because none of them could be true — or could they?

Saturday May 25
Feel a bit better after the Royal Society of Literature rejection. An outing on the disused railway line that is the Parkland Walk helps. I'm with Nicola and Vulcan plus our friend Paula and Labrador Livvy from Walthamstow. We walk from Finsbury Park through the old railway stations and bridges and stop for lunchtime chips at the Boogaloo pub in Highgate.

In the evening Nicola and myself go to see *Rocketman*, the Elton John biopic, at the Holloway Odeon. I'm pleased that lyricist Bernie Taupin comes out of it so well. Bernie inspired me to write. He was just 23 when *Goodbye Yellow Brick Road* came out. With me sitting by the Radiogram holding the gatefold sleeve of that album, reading the lyrics and looking at the fantastical illustrations and being introduced to a new world. I might not have attained world stardom like Bernie, but I've been published. My words made it somewhere. And my 14-year-old self would be impressed with that.

Sunday May 26
Nicola is cycling in her wetsuit to SUP (this stands for Stand-Up Paddleboarding) at the West Reservoir off Green Lanes. I've got used to her regular outfit of wetsuit, boots, cycling helmet and luminous jacket. Though I do fear the neighbours might be starting to regard seeing a cycling frogwoman as a tad unusual.

Go to see the Van Gogh exhibition at the Tate with

Nicola in the afternoon. Some of his starry starry nights are actually pictures of the Thames. Van Gogh famously cut off his ear — presumably while waiting for a Fiverr sale in the Dutch gig economy.

Monday May 27

It's a bank holiday and the foxes have been having another takeaway party in our garden. Ripped chip cartons, plastic bags and burger containers litter the area in front of the chicken coop. The girls next door are admiring the debris.

"The foxes must be getting really clever if they can order takeaways," I tell them. Nicola doesn't want to waste her bank holiday. "Bank holidays are for civilians," I tell her. "For us the muse never stops. Or indeed sometimes never starts."

I walk Vulcan and end our route with a cup of coffee in the cafe where Lola is working. She is good at dealing with the regulars, Geordie the postman, the lady who sings along to the music and doesn't like dogs, Andrew the dog lover and non-Corbynite from Plimsoll Road. Cut the hedge all afternoon — now summer is here the privet is showing Triffid-like growth patterns.

Tuesday May 28

"So this where the Wood Man lives?"

"Yes, it's come back to me now," says Nicola.

"We've got to tell him to stop. The cellar's overflowing! And it's too big to cut up."

Appropriately enough the Wood Man's front garden is completely covered in off-cuts of wood, much of it cut into mysterious curves and arches. Some of it is hardwood, plus paler woods, blocks and decking. Whatever he's doing in his house it's surely equivalent to the building of the *Mary Rose*. We tentatively knock. A

Hardy-esque man who looks like an aging Highbury hippy appears with a saw in his hand.

"We just wanted to say thanks for all the wood, it's really useful for our log burner, but we've got enough now and we don't have an electric saw," I mutter.

"But it's been really kind of you," adds Nicola.

"You don't want any more wood?" says the Wood Man, nonplussed.

"Not for the moment, but we'll let you know as soon as we've burned our way through what we have... maybe you could bring some more next year?"

The Wood Man looks genuinely puzzled that anyone could ever have too much wood. We feel like we have just cancelled his Christmas, but it had to be done.

After heartlessly chopping the Wood Man I return home to work on more music biographies. Then we head off to The Westbury where student daughter Lola is compering a pub quiz at her local in Turnpike Lane. I'm tremendously proud of Lola wielding the microphone with such confidence and displaying an effortless mastery of sporting, geographical and historical trivia. Never mind being a diplomat. She knows useless information. It doesn't get better than this.

Wednesday May 29

Finish reading our book club's choice, Sally Rooney's *Conversations With Friends*. Married man has an affair but doesn't leave his wife shocker. Rooney's humourless characters with their pseudy literary friends are really not very sympathetic, to my generation at least. Meanwhile Rosie tells us she is leaving to spend more time at home in Norwich after a very demanding job in London running an arts fair. We shall miss her bike and cheery personality. Our other lodger Monica is leaving too. She was very quiet and stayed in her room, perhaps not surprisingly as she was a psychologist who spent her days attending to the mental health issues of murderers. So we will have to decide on a replacement lodger or lodgers. It's nice to have all our rooms back, even if it is a blow to our cash flow. Cook sausage and mash for Nell to give her some A level comfort food.

Thursday May 30
Sold eight print copies and 12 e-books of *Man About Tarn* this month, plus two e-books of *Flying So High* and one e-book of *The Joy of Essex*. Made £47.76 in royalties from KDP plus $4.53 in the US market. Writing more potted music biographies. Punk rapper Sosmula is screaming murder and hollering about drugs, gangs and graves. A Brazilian rapper is sounding almost sweet by comparison and now there's a kind of French Billy Bragg-style protest singer.

At least writing the biographies gives me deadlines and a purpose, plus a weekly retainer of £50 to £70. Even if at my age I don't want to be in a gang. I'm sitting here in my late fifties watching drill videos, with much touting of guns and numerous humping lascivious female trophy bodies gyrating and twerking. Why are young drill rappers so insecure? Perhaps they could do with a session from life-coach Karen?

Friday May 31
Donald Trump is flying overhead. The chickens squawk. The dog rushes into the garden, tail bristling. "It's alright Vulcan, it's only Donald Trump," I announce matter-of-factly. There's the roar of three huge green military helicopters flying above us. A big man has a big chopper. Will there soon be the sound *Ride of the Valkyries*? I can feel the wind of the blades in my garden. "If I fall in the combat zone..." Still, I do make more money than

Donald if his old tax returns are accurate. The Donald is here to meet Theresa May. The whole house vibrates, probably making our subsidence worse. A car alarm goes off. It all feels very *Apocalypse Now* meets Finsbury Park.

Later we go to our local Park Theatre to see *The Last Temptation of Boris Johnson* by Jonathan Maitland. Much of the play takes place at an Islington dinner party, with Boris and his then-wife Marina Warner hosting Michael Gove, Sarah Vine and Evgeny Lebedev, the owner of the *Evening Standard,* on the night Boris opts to become a Brexiteer. In the play he finally makes it as Tory leader, becoming PM, but is then brought down by a scandal in his private life. A nice fantasy, but surely unlikely to happen in real life. Everyone knows this chancer has been found out.

JUNE

RUBBER CHICKEN HEIST — CONVERSATIONS WITH FRIENDS — DRINKS AT THE HOUSE — COLOSTOMY CATASTROPHE — AUTHOR, AUTHOR — DODD MAN OUT — EUROPEAN TOUR

Monday June 3

Nell is up at 6.30am as she has to be in for an A Level exam at nine. So a teenager can get up in the morning when motivated. It's a shock after her sometimes vampire-like late-night lifestyle, but she has revised hard and I'm impressed by her dedication. Qualifications my girl are what you need and then you might avoid the gig economy.

After Nell has left the house I take Nicola coffee in bed and retreat downstairs to let out the chickens. They are fine, but Vulcan's plastic chicken is missing. He sniffs for it with an air of puzzlement. I search all the rooms and the garden.

"Nicola!! The pesky fox has stolen Vulcan's chicken! It must have been left in the garden…"

"He's not meant to leave it out there…."

"He must have taken it out last night… when we left the French windows open."

The thing Vulcan loves most in the world is his plastic squeaking chicken. He managed to chew the last one to small shards of yellow plastic but was delighted when he received an identical replacement. The theft of it by the fox feels like a personal affront.

I sit on the seat in the garden musing on the ephemeral

existence of dog toys. Annie Dillard never wrote about this terrible side of nature. Poor Vulcan. But still, there are lovely white roses blooming above the chicken coop and blossom is all over the garden. It's been very hot over the weekend and we are lucky to have what is for London, a reasonable-sized garden to enjoy. I read some of Gerald Durrell's *My Family and Other Animals* in the sunshine and wonder what Theodore would make of our urban fox.

In the afternoon it's off to the London College of Communication for farewell drinks with the last batch of sports journalism students. I taught them blogging last year before I was made redundant. In truth it was always a strain performing in front of students. I did my best, but it's very hard to hold a class for two hours. The students are a good bunch, though the intake is down to single figures. Here are all the old lecturers. Anthony has left the *Sunday Mirror* and is now going full-time at Essex University. Huw is getting over his cancer and looking for new jobs. Mark is moving to the Journalism course. It's a nice crowd but after 12 years I still don't want to go into academia; foolishly I want to write books and do journalism rather than teach it.

Ping! Nell's A Level has gone well I learn from WhatsApp. After a drink or two at the student bar it's off to play for my pub quiz team the Beta Males at the Faltering Fullback. I'd probably fail a random alcohol test by this stage and perhaps it affects my game. We still hope that one day we will go pro and live on beer and crisps. But we come fourth, and another career opportunity disappears.

Tuesday June 4
Walk Vulcan who is still rather miserable without his rubber chicken. When I do my back exercises on the floor

he likes to savage the squeaking chicken and mate with a cushion, as dogs do.

Write a West Ham blog entry. Then two potted biographies of a US country singer and Finnish winner of *Idols,* earning £20. Work on a longer version of my 'Diary of a Writing Nobody' feature with the intention of trying it on a few publishers.

It's book group at our house with local readers Sue, Priti, Flicky, Dorothy, Anne, Ceinwen, John, Nicola and myself. Over wine, beer, crisps, hummus, cheese, bread, crackers and myriad other deli items we discuss *Conversations With Friends* by Sally Rooney. It must be a generation thing, but none of us like it much.

The book certainly gets over millennial themes. The characters spend a lot of time analysing emails and WhatsApp messages. It's well-written, a good portrait of a disturbed angst-ridden, unhappy person, but there's a lack of warmth. For an old git like me it's hard to like the characters. What are Melissa and Nick doing hanging out with students? While older man has affair with student and doesn't leave his wife is not that surprising a plot twist.

And there's no humour anywhere in the book. Does every scene have to take place at a book launch or a poetry reading or at a literary agent's? While I note that for all her anti-capitalist talk, Frances is quick to take the sum of 800 Euros she's offered for a short story by a literary magazine. But who is paying that kind of money today? Maybe things are different in Dublin.

Wednesday June 5
Do a music biography, walk Vulcan to Clissold Park. Spend all afternoon re-cutting our extensive front hedge, which is a surprisingly tiring activity in the sun. A lot more light is getting through to the house now thanks to

my work. Noel Coward had his *Private Lives* and I have my Privet Life.

Cook Nell a healthy dinner to get her through her politics A level tomorrow. At ten pm we hear a squeaking from the garden. It's the bloody fox with Vulcan's chicken.

"Quick, you go in the back garden and I'll head it off in the street," I tell Nicola, arming myself with a broom.

"Can you see it?" I shout from the street.

"No, it's gone off three gardens down, I can hear it playing with the chicken. Ah, it's sweet that foxes like to play too," says Nicola.

"No it isn't! Vulcan loved his chicken," I declare. A squeak echoes down the darkened gardens. "Don't think you'll get away with it. We'll be back!" I shout at the fox.

We retreat up to our bedroom. I read some Gerald Durrell in bed and wonder how anyone could live with such an eccentric family.

Thursday June 6

Today's *Guardian* headline claims that, "Ultimate limit of human endurance found". I thought it was being a freelance writer supporting West Ham. But it turns out the cap on human endurance is 2.5 times the body's resting metabolic rate, or 4000 calories a day for an average person. Anything more than that is not sustainable.

Vulcan initially refuses to walk with me to get the Growing Communities organic vegetables from the reservoir pick-up point in the afternoon. After a tugging battle over several streets I finally cajole him into action. It's a little worrying when a man is no longer master of his dog. Google for life details of a J-Pop rapper, which is surely a niche market. Do my Beta Males pub quiz match report. Nell's Politics A level has gone ok, she says.

Richard, Nicola's old friend from Yorkshire who is married to Fleur, stays with us overnight. He's a Yorkshire barrister who like his wife is a little out of place in Islington. Richard has been to a legal dinner at Lincoln's Inn, and talks to Nicola and myself about Debrett's and heraldry and a transitioning toff, Lady someone who is formerly a Lord. He says the heraldry people impale the crest for gay marriages, which sounds painful. Should I ever get a crest it will be a keyboard, a pint of beer and a publisher's rejection letter.

Friday June 7
Now the weather is hotter Nicola insists on propping open the French windows next to my desk with a boulder. She's forgotten that she is also exercising the chickens in the garden and they make a dash for my open office area. I shoo them out only to discover several round gloops of chicken poo in the area of my workstation. I end up on my knees with loo roll removing the fowl excrement and then shaking the rugs from the floor outside. My writing career is less Charles Dickens and more loose chickens.

Another message from Fiverr. "We haven't heard from you for a while…" My account is now paused, yet again. They are like a very demanding partner. I'm not going to reactivate the account now that I've got the music biography work. Finish writing the proposal-length version of my *Diary of a Nobody* idea.

Go to an exhibition on homelessness in Poland Street with Nicola then late-night viewing at the British Museum to see the Captain Cook exhibition before meeting Nell at Pizza Express to celebrate the fact she's only got one A level left. On our incomes eating out is a big treat.

Sunday June 9

Off to the Stoke Newington Literary Festival to see a talk on Alexander Baron and then do a Mary Wollstonecraft walk with Nell. Now there was a formidable writer who put Thomas Paine right with her *Vindication of the Rights of Woman*. Mary would have been out there with Nicola paddleboarding on the Grand Union Canal. She deserves the statue her supporters want to place on Newington Green.

Monday June 10

At breakfast Nell is convinced she has a cancerous growth on her face and goes to the doctor's. It turns out she has a large spot and not cancer. Surely this is a form of transference connected with exam anxiety.

Ben Bradman has asked me to write up two list pieces for the book being published by the wellness app CEO. Job done and £200 in the bag. Californian companies pay well.

Tuesday June 11

Now that I'm the poverty poster boy of the ALCS I've started to get invites to drinks at the House of Commons, hosted by the All-Parliamentary Writers Group. At the last one Tom Watson gave a speech before a vital Brexit vote and I saw the bête noire of my youth, a superannuated Norman Tebbit, no longer on his bike and instead looking like a nice old man.

This year the ALCS is announcing the results of its survey into writers' earnings, revealing that the average writers' annual income is now £10,437. It's gone down from £11,000 in 2013 and £12,330 in 2005. That's an average, meaning a lot of writers are earning less than £10k pa.

For a freelancer the event today is the chance of free drink and cakes and a slice of political glamour at the

House. I have to work for it though, queuing for 40 minutes to go through a metal detector and remove my belt and all metal objects in my pockets. Eventually it's through the great old hall and out to the rooms near the Thames terrace.

Without a plus one it's always difficult to know who to talk to, but I've mastered the art of moving from table to table looking like I know lots of literary types. I spot Caroline Sanderson who interviewed me for the *ALCS News* feature. We have a friendly chat, discussing West Ham and Leicester City's chances and I thank her for her piece. Moving on to work the room (or possibly get worked over by the room) I'm pleased to unexpectedly find Michael McManus, the political author and playwright; we sit together at West Ham matches and both share a love of *Doctor Who*.

Michael's carrying the programme of *Tainted*, his musical featuring the music of Mark Almond. It's had a one-off outing at Heaven and Michael is now looking for a backer. He's also had a political play about populism performed this year, *An Honourable Man* that ran for a week at the White Bear. Once the cost of hiring actors and the theatres have been accounted for it's cost him a lot of money. Like most of us he's taking a big gamble, hoping that someone will step in and decide that he is still a contender. Though at 59 I'm not sure if I count as a hip young gunslinger anymore... We move on to discussing West Ham's transfer policy amid the cakes and clinking wine glasses, before meeting Baroness someone-or-other who is writing a book on women and the environment.

There are speeches by John Whittingdale MP and others, which bemoan the annual incomes for those in the creative industries. As I'm about to leave I discover from his laminated name card that I've bumped into James McConnachie, editor of the Society's of Author's magazine *The Author* — the very man who is publishing my 'Diary of a Writing Nobody' feature. He proves to be really friendly and after I mention my idea of extending it into a book, he says it reminded him of *The Diary of a Bookseller* by Shaun Bythell and suggests a couple of contacts at Profile books. So much of writing is about contacts and it's always better to meet an editor face to face.

I leave the House in a wine-induced haze, strolling past policemen and through a security turnstile and on to Westminster tube station. For an evening at least I have joined the metropolitan liberal elite.

Wed June 13

"Dad, there's a snail in the shower! This wouldn't happen in any other house..." complains Nell in the morning. "Well don't complain too loudly or everyone will want one," I reply. "It must have come in through the French windows. I'll liberate it in the garden."

Do two more music biographies today, of Joyner Lucas (whose song *I'm Not Racist* is both caustic but also aware of what drives Trump supporters) and J-Pop star Celeina Ann. Make Nell dinner and then Nicola and myself head out to watch *Private Lives* while sitting on straw bales in the rain at Freightliners City Farm. It's an annual fundraising event for the farm. Outdoor theatre is always fun when accompanied by the cries of a cockerel. The other year the farm put on *Romeo and Juliet* as a play about two knife-wielding gangs, which greatly interested the local Holloway kids.

Thursday June 14

A call from Ben Bradman at 9am. He wants me to do a morning's work thinking up ideas for something promoted by John McEnroe. You can not be serious!

Jerk! Ben takes my McEnroe jokes well, until I tell him that he is the pits of the world.

Do a blog on the announcement of West Ham's fixtures for the news season. Nell arrives home having finally finished her A levels. She's worked hard and hopefully she'll get good grades, though we'll love her whatever they are. She goes off to celebrate with her peers at the 'Spoons, aka the Mossy Well In Muswell Hill.

Sunday June 16
We go out for a family dinner with Nicola, Lola and Nell on a barge-restaurant, which is moored on the canal by Paddington station. The restaurant is atmospheric and the food is excellent. We congratulate Nell on getting through her A levels and Lola on finishing her second year at SOAS. We return home and Nell goes round to her friend Ruth's house to continue her celebrations.

Monday June 17
Nell got in at 4 am, as you do. We have slept uneasily. A text message trail reveals various entreaties to get her home from 'Jem's House'. Jem's house is where her coterie of sixth-formers chooses to hang out, Jem's house seeming to be stationed above a time rift and Jem seeming to have a dad who doesn't believe in time boundaries. When Lola was in the sixth form we had similar problems with 'Daisy's House', a party venue that made the Kit-Kat club in *Cabaret* seem a bit straight-laced.

Down to the doctor's surgery for a blood test, as Dr Klopp is worried about a possible vitamin D deficiency. Though the more blood tests you have, the more things they seem to turn up. My blood is surely mainly Arabica. I have a coffee on the way back at Rohan's cafe, where

Lola is working.

It's going to be a busy summer. Nicola's mum Fiona has turned 80 and has invited her family to stay at a luxury holiday home in Sarlat in the Dordogne next month. Meanwhile Nell has planned an Inter-Rail trip with Ruth, Orla and Isabella, which has involved a lot of pre-booking and a route that has seen her end up in Budapest — although she also wants to go to granny's 80th celebrations in Sarlat, which involves getting to Bordeaux. You couldn't have chosen two places further apart. She won't be able to make it by train and Nicola is ethically opposed to booking a flight. So I spend three hours trying to book Nell a flight from Budapest to Bordeaux, hoping her mum won't notice.

This is very difficult as the only direct flight seems to leave at 6.30am in the morning. And there's some doubt about whether she arrives in Budapest at ten in the morning or the evening. Eventually I find an internet airline company offering flights from Budapest to Amsterdam and then Amsterdam to Bordeaux and book it for a stonking £230. We haven't flown since 2011 due to climate change guilt, and confusingly the company just issues a booking number not a ticket. I start to worry if I've been conned and if my daughter will be marooned and sold into modern slavery. Not that I receive gratitude from my slightly hungover teenager.

Compile a final music biography, cook dinner and watch *Love Island* with Nicola and Nell, having finally persuaded her to spend an evening at home.

Tuesday June 18
Do three music biographies. Email the insurers about arranging a subsidence meeting. Send an invoice for my PR work on the wellness app. Make a birthday card for Lola, printing out some old photos of her and some Billy

Bragg/Paul Simon lyrics about her being 21 years when she wrote this song.

Wednesday June 19
There's a good piece on declining writers' incomes in the *Guardian* by Alison Flood headlined: "There's no safety net: The plight of the midlist author." It points out that only five per cent of writers earn the income that Virginia Woolf argued was needed to work — today about £30,000pa. The piece talks to two writers who have published more than ten books each, both of whom have been struggling. It mentions the All Party Parliamentary Writers Group's survey, which has found that writers' incomes have fallen by 42 per cent since 2005 and the problem of midlist writers suffering from minimal marketing budgets while debuts get huge budgets. There's also the sobering figure that 184,000 books are published a year in the UK, so it's perhaps not a surprise that most authors are midlist rather than in the J K Rowling league.

Meanwhile Rosie our low-impact lodger leaves to return home to Norwich. She gives us a beautiful framed lino cut of a kitchen table that she has made, so we must have done something right. We'll miss her. And she was very tolerant of Nicola placing a paddling pool in her shower so that she could save the water for the garden. As is customary with our hardy lodgers, I present her with two signed copies of my books, *There's a Hippo In My Cistern* and *The Joy of Essex*. After all, I do have a lot of them in the attic.

Thursday June 20
"Aaaaagh! There's a colostomy bag in the garden!" shouts Nicola at breakfast. "The bloody fox has left a colostomy bag by the chicken coop."

"How do you know?" I ask.

"I know what they look like. There's wee in it. And a tube! Who puts colostomy bags in their rubbish?"

"It could be a very ill fox," I suggest.

"I can't touch it, it's revolting! You'll have to do it. And don't keep talking about it, it will put me off my breakfast!'"

Our friend Paula is staying as her flat in Leyton is being used by a Canadian family, as she's joined a family house swap website. Nicola has been in the garden letting the chickens out of their inner coop. Paula looks dubiously at her toast. She has inadvertently found herself staying with Mr and Mrs Edvard Munch.

"You're a farmer's son, you'll be fine. And don't use my gardening gloves!" adds Nicola.

I find an ancient blue rubber glove under the sink and survey the scene of detritus over our garden from my office window. I'm pretty sure that all the modern writers I admire, like Nick Hornby, David Nicholls, and Stuart Maconie, don't have to put up with plastic sachets of urine being deposited in front of their workplace.

Gingerly I pick up the colostomy bag by the tube and place it in a black bin liner. There's a horrible smell of acidic old urine. Thank goodness it's not full of anything worse. Then I scoop up other bits of detritus, chip cartons, ripped plastic bags, unspecified pieces of red wrappers, and a nappy. I run through the kitchen with the bag full of horrors as Nicola ushers me through and out of the front door towards the fox-proof dustbin.

Returning to my desk I manage to write one musical biography of an Argentine trap singer. At 2pm Nell, who has again been over-celebrating the end of her A levels, gets up. She has to finalise her Inter-Rail itinerary, we tell her.

"Could you put my coffee in the microwave. And can

I go to a barbecue at five?" says Nell.

"But you didn't get home until two am and we were exchanging texts at 1.30!"

"I won't be late."

"That's what you said last night. You will."

"I'm going anyway."

We persuade her to check train times from Bordeaux to Berlin for an hour.

"There's a poo stuck in the loo!" shouts Nicola at 3pm.

"Well, use the jug of water!"

"I can't, I've got to teach riding now," says Nicola. "Sorry. You're not having a good day are you?"

Our upstairs loo has a poor flush and this sort of thing often happens. So I walk upstairs and pour a jug of water over the offending turd. Eventually it flushes away.

I set off to go to bank and get some Euros and Hungarian Forints for Nell.

A woman saunters up to Nell and myself as we wait for the W7 at the bus station.

"Can you spare some money please, I'm pregnant!"

"I haven't got any money I'm a journalist!" I say, rattily.

"But journalists make lots of money!"

"No they don't. It's a dying industry!" I declare.

The begging woman moves down the bus queue looking for someone else to touch for the price of a cup of tea. Has it come to this? Dodging colostomy bags in my garden, tackling unsinkable giant turds and now arguing with the homeless at Finsbury Park bus station? It's been that sort of day.

Friday June 20

A much better day. *The Author* arrives with my 'Diary of a Nobody' feature inside. I tear open the plastic envelope with a feeling of excitement. It's been a long time since something has actually made it into a printed magazine. Even better they paid me the £250 when it was commissioned, not on publication as is customary. It looks great, a piece with gravitas in a serious magazine written for writers by writers.

Relentless self-publicising also goes with the job description of writer. I tweet an image of the article and then share a scan of it on my Facebook page. "The modern Charles Pooter on the less glamorous side of being a jobbing writer..." As Kate Bush once sang, *Don't Give Up...* There are even some positive tweets. "Just read your diary article in The Author and had to tell you it's brilliant and made me laugh (and relate). Have a good weekend!" writes Kitiara, a travel writer and author of *In Bed With The Atlantic*. Maybe I have started a movement...

Saturday June 22
It's a daily battle with clinical waste. Inspect the garden and find a plastic tube from the colostomy bag that I missed yesterday. I pick it up while wearing Nicola's gardening gloves and deposit it in our dustbin.

Just as well I've cleared the garden of its dystopian refuse, as we're having a garden brunch to celebrate Lola's 21st birthday. She arrives with her usual entourage of three male acolytes from SOAS. Granny Fiona is impressed. "I thought you'd given up on boys, Lola," says Fiona. "But Granny, they haven't given up on me," replies Lola.

Lola seems pleased with the yellow Hunter waterproof jacket that we've bought her as an attempt to entice her back to the Lake District. We feast on all sorts of treats before Lola returns to Turnpike Lane for more socialising.

Was it really 21 years ago today that I left Nicola in hospital as visiting hours had ended at 8pm and rushed home to see England lose to Romania in the World Cup, celebrating with a can of beer regardless. It's gone both slowly and quickly and now my tiny baby daughter is a woman. Hopefully I've been a good dad even if I did ruin her life by taking her to West Ham games.

June 23— June 28

I'm off on a five-day sojourn in the Lake District. It's unusually hot for the Lakes, but taking advantage of the long days I manage to set out at 5pm on my arrival at Keswick and bag Dodd. Eight new Wainwright fells are completed over four days so it's a productive trip. I get to sample the boggy delights of Wainwright's least favourite mountain, Armboth Fell, which is one to impress the anoraks and my pal Nigel; view the idyllic gleaming Watendlath Tarn (which has a tea room); finally conquer Eagle Crag and Sergeant Crag; sample the quieter charms of the northern fells on Souther Fell and Bannerdale Crags.

On my final morning it's 27C and it's so hot that I can hardly stagger up the steep incline of Great Mell Fell. On the summit I meet a man who once repaired a hurdy-gurdy for Pete Townshend, which is a first. It's all much better than writing music biographies.

While I'm there the father of one of my old editors, Bill, has left me a message on my phone about taking over a monthly Pilates newsletter, which sounds interesting, even if I am to wellness what Jose Mourinho is to diplomacy.

Saturday June 29

Back in sweltering London from the Lakes and it's off

with Nicola to our friend Richard's 70th birthday party on a boat cruising down the Thames. We see London Bridge open and travel down to the Thames Barrier and back again as the guests drink cold beer and try to avoid getting sunburnt on deck. Lots of old faces from our book group and the girls' old school are there and it's a very pleasant voyage in the sun.

We get back from the party to discover that Nell is in the park with her friends and still showing no signs of packing for her Inter-Rail trip tomorrow. Several irate texts force her to return home and start packing at nine pm. Fail to prepare, prepare to fail as numerous Roy Keane-like characters have declared. Check my KDP charts. Sold 12 print books and 11 e-books on KDP this month, earning £52 in royalties.

Sunday June 30
We wake up at five am, as Nicola is escorting Nell to Victoria coach station where she's setting off with Ruth on the 7.30am coach for Paris. In Paris they are meeting Orla and Isabella. Nell sets off with a giant back-pack and my thoughts turn to my own Inter-Rail memories back in 1979; of getting a train to Madrid and finding it split in half at night and ending up in Valencia, of sleeping outside Rome station because we arrived too late to find a hotel; being woken up by gun-toting guards on a private beach in Venice; the football-stadium like arena of the Coliseum; that wondrous climb up to the Acropolis in Athens.

Only at 7.15 am I receive a phone call from Nicola. She's unusually calm and speaking in slow considered sentences, which means something terrible has gone wrong. Nell has remembered her passport, Euros and Hungarian cash but has forgotten her actual Inter-Rail pass. Apparently she didn't think she needed it. Ruth is in tears. Nicola asks me to book a later coach ticket.

After some cursing and slapping of my head I boot up my computer and miraculously manage to book a pair of coach tickets to Paris for £50 each. I print them out. A sheepish Nell returns to the house with a slightly less-tearful Ruth. I give them the tickets and send them back to Victoria where Nicola is waiting with their backpacks. By some miracle they get on the coach.

I slump with my head in my hands. Soldiers have returned from the combat zone in Iraq with less post-traumatic stress disorder issues than I am experiencing. How will my teenage daughter ever get round Europe?

JULY

LAUGHING GAS — MONEY FOR NOTHING —
BIG IN THE LAKES — PARISIAN HEIST —
DORDOGNE DAZE — CHEQUE MATE — BATH
TIME — RETURN OF THE RUBBER CHICKEN

Monday July 1

It's going to be busy summer. We have ten days in France booked to celebrate Nicola's mum's birthday. My sister Pam is over from Australia and staying with us for four weeks so she can be here for my 60th birthday. She booked several months ago to get a cheap flight on the new non-stop service. She'll be staying with me for all the four weeks, rather than spending some time at my other sister Kaz's house, whose new house in Essex is in a permanent state of re-plastering.

Trips to Bath and Kings Lynn have been booked and I'll show Pam around London as much as I can. While at the end of August our family have a week booked at a cottage in Keswick. It's going to be an expensive summer but this is my 60th year and it seems the right time to dip into some more of the capital that my parents left me when my they died back in 2006-2007. Ideally I'd like to leave some of that capital to my children, but in reality it could be used up getting me through to the state pension age of 66.

A boost arrives on twitter. Crime fiction writer Marion Todd comments, "Loved your Diary of a Writing Nobody in Society of Authors journal. I'm off to investigate *Man About Tarn.*' I tweet my heartfelt thanks.

Tuesday July 2

Go to scatter some corn for the chickens and discover a large dead black-feathered object in front of their coop. For a moment I fear it might be one the bantams that I've forgotten to lock-up at night. But a closer look reveals it to be a dead crow, splayed like some terrible symbol of doom on the wood chips. It's all very Ted Hughes, though this is north London and not rural Yorkshire.

Flies are buzzing around its eyes, which reminds me of the lyrics of Bob Dylan's *Idiot Wind*. It has no obvious signs of being eaten. There are three possible culprits. Joe the cat from next door, the large black cat that travels through our garden and the fox family. Unless the crow has just dropped from the sky with some terrible avian disease, that is now going to infect us all. I take a shovel and deposit the deceased bird into a black bin-liner. Then I place it in the dustbin, as Nicola doesn't want it in her compost. Though it's tempting to leave it to decompose in the front hedge where at least the smell might put off the miscreants who wait to complete Class A drug deals on our street corner.

After being diverted by my temporary duties as a funeral director I return to work and write two potted profiles of Jamaican producer and singer Rvssian (yes he does spell his name like that) and French rap outfit 47ter. Talk to Bill on the phone about what the Pilates newsletter would entail. All I know about Pilates is that successful people in Hollywood do it, but it would be useful money. I did try a couple of lessons a decade ago, but ended up putting my back out.

Nicola does a phone interview with a 17-year-old from Morocco (who is the cousin of a school governor) about staying in our house while he tries to get in to university, as she is panicking about Nell leaving and has early empty nest syndrome. I'm not sure about this as he's not sure to get into uni and we'd be acting as surrogate parents.

Do two blog posts and make one pence in revenue on AdSense. Nell sends a WhatsApp message from Barcelona, so at least they have made it to Spain. Try to find some contacts at Profile Books — why do publishing websites never put up commissioning editors' emails? Do they want books or not? I know there are no-hopers, but it's difficult to find who to send something to even if you are an established writer.

Wednesday July 3
Take Vulcan for a walk to Clissold Park. On the way back from an Americano with cold milk at the Clissold House café I find a £20 note lying on the path. This feels like being a character in *Crime and Punishment*. Does a good life make up for a bad act? I pick up the £20, consoling myself with the thought that it might have been dropped by a shareholder in a major publisher.

Thursday July 4
Lakeland Walker arrives in the post, containing my feature on walking with kids. It's great to see something in print and a big psychological boost. The editor emails to say he likes my bus idea too and might be up for a column. Then he adds that his budget is in doubt and everything has to go on hold for a couple of months. A pyrrhic victory, I think they call it. Do a blog post and two music biogs, including Dave Bartholomew, who is interesting. Arrange to meet Bill at his Pilates studio to discuss the newsletter job.

Friday July 5
Invoice for my music biographies. The subsidence battle rages on as our insurers email to refuse a meeting with

our own independent engineer, Martin. Buy a new portfolio from the stationers, stepping through the wobbling flesh of Wireless festivalgoers in Finsbury Park. All the women seem to be in micro shorts and everyone has glitter on their faces.

Return home with my new portfolio book. It's always satisfying to fill a new portfolio with printed features that I have written and so I carefully cut out my *Lakeland Walker* and *Author* features and slide them into the plastic folders. I started filling up my first writer's portfolio in 1986 and now have 23 of them, containing everything I've ever written.

Sunday July 7
The street is full of discarded laughing gas cylinders from the Wireless crowd. Parking is restricted, but the drug dealers have still moved into our closed roads as they presumably class themselves as local residents, suggests Nicola. In fact one of her writers on *Pavement*, says that outside our house was a well-known pick-up point for his Class-A drug deals.

In the afternoon it's drinks and food at Carolyn and David's house to celebrate their daughter Corinna's MA. When we're back home Khalid from next door calls round to talk about the subsidence claim he is also making. Another neighbour Adrian comes past and says they had subsidence too and had their bay window underpinned. As property prices soar our houses collapse around us.

Monday July 8
Put the rubbish in the dustbin and discover a terrible smell from the decaying dead crow inside a bin liner. Nicola insists on picking up the corpse bag and placing it inside the second bin bag in case the bin men don't take

both bags and we get maggots. Nature is red in tooth and claw and dustbins in Finsbury Park.

Head off down Upper Street to meet Bill at his Pilates studio. He's in his 90s and a great advert for Pilates as he looks very fit and is still running the studio himself. He's spent most of his career in the theatrical world before that. Though Bill does take issue with my posture and tells me not to slouch. He introduces me to some teachers, then shows me what seem to be various medieval torture devices in the studio and a collection of photos of Joseph Pilates on the wall. We have a pleasant chat and I agree to take on the newsletter next month. Do I want to be writing about Pilates? I'm not that sure as I'm no expert, but I have to get some income from somewhere and it might even help me get fit.

In the evening play for the Beta Males in the Faltering Fullback's pub quiz and we finish a disappointing mid-table. We perform well on the quiz questions, but are eventually undone by the picture round, which contains ten fiendishly difficult anagrams of Arnold Schwarzenegger films such as *Conan the Barbarian*, *Kindergarten Cop* and *Red Sonya*. But at least a lengthy credit has to go to our captain Bob for deducing that *hippopotomonstrosesquippedaliophobia* is the fear of long words.

Tuesday July 9
Better news is that I completed a book deal last night, with Captain Bob from the pub quiz team requesting a signed West Ham tome for his mate Keith and paying cash up front. I walk to Finsbury Park Post Office to mail him a copy of *Goodbye to Boleyn*, only the street is taped off and the Post Office closed because of a shooting and stabbing last night. Some people take losing the pub quiz very badly. So I take the bus to Crouch End and post a

signed copy from there — not many authors would dodge bullets to get Bob's mate Keith a book. Write a further three music biogs, and as research watch videos of groups of men loafing around with guns and ornamental women who seem to have forgotten to get dressed.

Friday July 12
Take Vulcan to Sue and Richard's house, where he is staying during our trip to France. Sell another copy of *Man About Tarn* to pub-quizzer Adrian, meeting him round the back of the local FE college to take his cash. Do a music biog, Hoover the floors, pack for France. Around ten o'clock at night we rush out as we can hear the pesky fox playing with Vulcan's squeaking chicken. We try to ambush the fox outside as squeaks come from our neighbours' gardens and people are looking out of windows. It's as if it's taunting us before we go away.

Saturday July 13 - Monday July 22
We're off on the Eurostar on our way to Sarlat, for Nicola's mum Fiona's birthday celebrations. Nell is meeting us there if she can successfully catch her flight from Budapest. Last-minute work has been completed and we can finally relax. Nicola and myself take a celebratory selfie over morning coffee. At Gare du Nord we meet eldest daughter Lola, and it's exciting for us all to be in Paris again, where Lola lived for a year when she was working as a nanny during her gap year.

We have to rush on the Metro to get to Gare Saint-Lazare, as we only have 40 minutes to make the train to Bordeaux. I'm also worried about Nell making her flight. We're in a packed compartment but eventually get a fold down seat. I keep one eye on our bags as a text from Nell comes through. She has made it on the flight to Amsterdam and is waiting for her second flight to

Bordeaux. In my head she is still seven, but actually she seems to be better at travel than me. We hastily disembark at Gare St Lazare as the doors swoosh open.

We have 15 minutes to make the train, which is fine. But as I step on to the Metro platform there's an empty feeling in my pocket where there should be something solid. Where is it? My wallet has gone... oh no. Sod it. Nicola says she saw a dodgy looking person, I felt someone bump against me at one point when I was standing. Lola says the Parisian pickpockets are experts. I'm wearing shorts and I should have zipped up that pocket but I was so busy worrying about whether Nell had caught her flight and excited to see Lola and worried about making the train connection that I acted like a dolt.

Luckily my passport is in a valuables bag round my neck, but my wallet contained 210 Euros in cash. It's a lot of cash. That's 21 bloody music biographies I've written for nothing. Now the proceeds of all that labour have gone to a Parisian heroin addict. Plus my wallet contained my driving licence and my credit and debit cards, not to mention my Society of Authors card, though frankly a Parisian tea-leaf will find this doesn't take them too far in terms of easy money. If the thief is cultured they will also have access to National Trust and English Heritage properties and the British Museum through my other cards. They might even be able to hack into my miniscule royalties.

We have to rush on to the train to Bordeaux and I slump at my seat in misery, before phoning Nat West to cancel my cards. Nicola buys me a cold beer from the buffet, which helps a little. I'm going to have to rely on her for money for the rest of the trip.

At Bordeaux we walk down somnolent sunny streets to find our Air B&B rooms, in the attic of a real French person's house, complete with a big door, tiled lobby, shaded stairs and a Mediterranean ambience. We have a good pizza in a restaurant near the lovely cathedral, all glowing yellow stone in the evening light. At 10.30pm Nicola takes an Uber to the airport and miraculously turns up with Nell, tottering beneath a huge backpack. The family is reunited. Things feel a little better.

After a night in Bordeaux we take the Sunday train to Sarlat and arrive at a holiday home way beyond our normal budget. It has a swimming pool amid a giant garden and immaculate rooms. Every bedroom has a designer bathroom and showers with three types of jet. Even better there is a giant Lidl nearby, so it's not too different to Finsbury Park.

We're joined my brother-in-law Drew, his wife Kate and children Jago and Rose, plus Granny Fiona and her partner Anthony. With a borrowed laptop I manage to transfer Nicola some money and I then live off her handouts of cash.

After a terrible start it's a fine week. It's only money and plastic that has been lost. Sarlat is a wonderful medieval town, full of alleyways and charming shops. We watch fireworks go off on Bastille Day. For a couple of days our family hire bikes and cycle 20 miles to the river Dordogne, with its clear water full of bathers and towering white limestone cliffs. We drive to towns perched above giant cliffs such as Dome and take a cruise to see La Roque Saint Christophe, a town that is built into the ancient cliffs.

We visit the caves at Lascaux thanks to the car drivers and see reproductions of the marvellous cave art from 30,000 years ago. The sun is fierce and we end the days in the swimming pool, drifting on inflatables before eating communal food and wine on the terrace.

We leave via another train to Bordeaux and a 38C heatwave. Predictably Nicola has booked us on a cycling tour of the city in the morning. We speed round the old town, via vast old churches, and see the developing south bank. It's an impressive city and Lola puts it on her list of places to live. We see Nell off as she catches the train to Berlin to continue her Inter-Railing. I tell her to guard her wallet. After a hasty and illicit shower in the hotel's gym it's out to the sweltering station and the 17.04 train to Paris followed by the 21.13 Eurostar train to London. I arrive home at 11 o'clock to find new credit and debit cards in the mail and that my sister has arrived from Australia and picked up a key from our good neighbours (which everybody needs).

Tuesday July 23

Back to toiling at the typeface. Say hello to my jetlagged elder sister Pam and welcome her to Pommieland. She's arrived with the largest suitcase in the world, containing her own pillow and enough clothes for a decade. She's lived in Australia since she was 19 or so and we only get to catch up every four years or so, though I did stay with her in Oz during my backpacking days and before a trip to the Solomon Islands with Nicola and the girls back in 2011.

The fox has left a disposable nappy in the back garden and some shreds of white plastic bags and foil takeaway containers. My task is to clear this up. Nicola fetches Vulcan from his holiday at Sue and Richard's house and he immediately rushes out into the garden to tilt at foxes.

We unpack and I hastily go to the bank to pay in a cheque for £175 from *Lakeland Walker* that has arrived in the post — possibly the last magazine in the western world still to pay by cheque, but I'll take any form of payment.

The tap at the kitchen sink that was dripping a bit

before we left has become much worse during our absence, inflicting us with a kind of water torture. So we book a plumber for the next day.

Do a West Ham blog update and then start work on the seven music biographies for this week. I have to complete them before a trip to Bath with my sisters on Thursday.

It's best to keep some form of income coming in while I'm entertaining my sister for the next month. This week's biogs are American country singer Chris Lane, J-Pop stars Yusuke and Kana Nishino, South Korean singer HEIZE, British house artist Joel Corry and American rapper Tyle Yaweh. Plus Welsh band Pretty Vicious, who prove to be really good in a thoroughly anti-social way — their single *Cave Song* is one of the best things I've heard since the Sex Pistols.

Wednesday July 25

The tap is now a stream. A taciturn Welsh plumber arrives and mutters about the tap being a German design, but eventually leaves to get parts and returns with a British tap and a bill for £200. Nicola complains that I have bought cheap tomatoes from Sainsbury. Rather testily I mutter about my wallet being nicked, the deposit for the holiday cottage in the Lakes, the plumber's bill, Nell's flight and Nell's extra coach, and suggest that tomato austerity is an economic necessity. Rush to complete my remaining four music biographies in time for dinner.

Thursday July 25 - Saturday July 27

Take the train to Bath with my sisters Pam and Kaz. Nicola is staying at home with Vulcan and Nell. I'm not earning as much as either of them, but as Pam is only here every four years we splash out on single rooms in an £80 a night B & B, which is a rare luxury. It's good to have no work pressure for three days. It's a stifling 37C when we arrive and walk down the hill to look round the town. The next day we do a guided tour, take in the Roman baths and Georgian crescents, wallow in the thermal baths for the afternoon, eat a pub dinner and return the following day.

Sunday July 28
Nell has returned from Inter-Railing. In my day it was sleeping outside Rome station and being chased off the beach in Venice by gun-wielding guards. But Nell's generation seem to have a much more luxurious Air B&B lifestyle. She's clubbed in Berlin, stayed by pristine blue Italian lakes and made it to the referendum voter's destination of choice, Split.

We host a garden barbecue in her honour, complete with her friends Nita and Ruth. Ruth missed her flight back from Amsterdam because of a late night clubbing. So it's not just my teenager who has Inter-Railing punctuality problems. Lola is here with her student entourage. My pal Nigel pops in with his West Ham season ticket for the Man City game. I do a good job on the barbecue with my mix of veggie and meat sausages. It's a balmy night and my beer tastes good. If the kids are united, then we'll never be divided.

As the shadows lengthen and the mosquitoes start to bite, we hear squeaking emanating from Vulcan's stolen rubber chicken. Is the fox still taunting us? This time it's a few doors down our road. "I think it's at Mike and the twins' garden," says Nicola. She races round there, disappears for 20 minutes and returns triumphantly holding the rubber chicken.

"The fox had left it in their garden, and Mike's dog had adopted it," explains Nicola. "They were glad to get rid of it as it had been driving them mad!"

"Brilliant! Look Nell, we've got our chicken back! It's one small step for Vulcan, one giant squeak for dogkind!"

Vulcan is ecstatic to get his rubber chicken back and immediately starts to harry it while mating with a cushion. Nicola and myself are shouting, "He's got his chicken, he's got his chicken!" Nell wonders why the Europeans regard the English as slightly crazed.

Monday July 29

Nicola has placed an ad for a lodger on spareroom.co.uk. "We are looking for someone who takes environmental issues seriously. We have a dog and two chickens and are mainly vegetarian. Lots of the furniture and furnishings are patched which we think gives our home character and damages the planet less. This is a busy house — we are not tidy and we never will be." That should get rid of most applicants. Our prospective lodgers must be imagining *The Good Life* merged with *Steptoe and Son* and *The Young Ones*.

Send my book proposal to three publishers and agents. Genius is 99 per cent perspiration and I've almost mastered that bit. Apply for a replacement driving licence and numerous other cards that were half-inched in Paris.

In the evening we go to see *The Hunt* at the Almeida, a well-acted but not very uplifting Scandinavian play about a man wrongly accused of being a paedophile. All very Nordic noir. Still, it's nice to show Pam something of Islington culture.

Tuesday July 30

Nicola's Islington Faces exhibition is moving to a new venue, with Kimi's pictures of Nicola's interview subjects now being hung at the Ringcross Community Centre, near Holloway Road. The whole family attend along with various friends and Nicola makes a speech. The evening ends with two of her subjects on stage, Hanisha performing her Ethiopian songs and Stanley, one of the first Trinidadian migrants to arrive in Islington and now in his eighties, singing *Moon River*. It's very moving.

Wednesday July 31
Made £45.37 from KDP royalties this month, selling 12 print and eight e-books of *Man About Tarn,* plus two copies of *Whovian Dad* and one copy of *Sunday Muddy Sunday.* Complete my West Ham pre-season answers for the *Observer's* fans round-up. It's another unpaid gig (years ago they did used to pay me for diary items and the odd piece in *Observer Sport*) but there's still some kudos in seeing my byline in a national newspaper, plus a plug for my West Ham blog and book *Goodbye to Boleyn.* Complete three out of five music biographies before catching the train to Kings Lynn with my sisters.

AUGUST

**NORFOLK ENCHANTS — ROOM TO LET — THE
A LEVEL TEAM — LITERARY FEEDBACK —
ROMAN ESSEX — 60 NOT OUT — ALBERTO
PONCE — KEEP TAKING THE PILATES —
CANAL KNOWLEDGE**

Wednesday August 1 — Thursday August 2

Spend the day in Kings Lynn with my sisters. Our parents retired to Lynn in 1984 and for 20 years this was the place we all went to see them. It's still odd to arrive at the station and not see them waiting on the platform, my dad in his cap, my mum in her red coat. Their house was sold a decade ago, but when we visit it still looks the same from outside and I half expect to see my mum and dad in the garden.

We visit my parents' grave in the peaceful churchyard of their village. The gravestone needs some nettles clearing and a scrub to remove some bird poo. I like the fact it has a quote from Robert Burns on it. My mum was always very supportive about writing, and I recall her excitement at ordering my first book at W H Smith.

My dad wanted me to be a farmer like him and take over his tenant farm. It was never for me. He saw writing very much in financial terms and told me to go and work for Rupert Murdoch because he was shaking up the trade unions — not something a young leftie would ever want to do. It was hard to explain that seeing my name on a book spine meant more than money. My mum said he was secretly proud of me, though the closest he got to saying so was when he said that *Hammers in the Heart* was a good book a few years before he died. I'm not sure if he would be impressed that I am still hanging on as a self-employed writer, or dismayed that my income has gone steadily down along with most of the industry.

Still, I gave it a shot and published 15 books. One piece of luck, an agent who didn't dump me, one book published at the right time, one review in the right place, one editor who didn't leave might have yielded a best-seller. Yet they were published and that's an achievement — and I'm not giving up yet.

After the graveyard visit we eat out in Kings Lynn and I research the career of Tyler Childers on my phone for one of my biographies and take some notes. He's impressive, country Americana with real emotion. The next day we visit the purple fields of Norfolk Lavender. I spent a year up here in 2008, on and off, sorting out my dad's estate at weekends, dealing with endless accounts and stocks and shares and a mountain of furniture. But Lynn still has its sleepy charms, the Guildhall, the Customs House, the wide grey expanse of the Wash — it's a welcome break from London and a chance to reflect on mortality.

Friday August 2
Return to London at lunchtime. Nicola wants me to pump up the tyres of two bikes, which is an inflationary pressure I can do without. Write up the Tyler Childers biography (he's interviewed in the *Guardian* today which makes me feel vaguely on trend) and then research a Dutch cello player Anner Bylsma, about whom I know absolutely nothing. Classical and jazz artists are the biographies I struggle with, but I'm getting better at affecting a bluffer's air of expertise.

In the garden Nicola proudly serves up her homegrown spinach and feta filo pastry pie for dinner. It tastes very good to me, though Nell has found a problem. "Mum, that's a caterpillar!"

"No, it's just a stalk," mutters Nicola, eyeing up the offending item hesitantly. "Oh, maybe it is... Well you are a meat eater!"

"And humans might eventually have to rely on insects for protein," I add. Nell has been expert at finding hairs and unspecified objects in her food since she was tiny.

"And that's a spider!" she adds. "I'm making some toast!"

If there is a name for a caterpillar-induced eating disorder, we have probably just given it to Nell.

Sunday August 4
Wake Nell up at 10.30 with a coffee in bed after a knock on her door and cry of "Room Service!" Then I ask: "Would madam like her caterpillars lightly sautéed or well-done for breakfast?" Nell smiles and goes back to looking at her phone.

As we are now minus a lodger, Nicola has put a request out on Facebook among her Solomon Island circles. She worked with VSO in the Solomon Islands for two years in the 1990s and I've visited twice with her since. I'm fairly used to Solomon Islanders turning up in London at our house and Nicola speaking in Pijin. The Pacific Island Society have seen the post and introduced her to Frieda, from Papua New Guinea, who needs a short-term let while she works at the PNG High Commission. She comes over for a chat, and seems nice when we interview her, so we offer her the room.

Monday August 5
Summer rain. Frieda emails to say she has taken up an alternative offer. Never mind, our cluttered terminally untidy house is not for everyone and I wasn't sure about a

full-time lodger. A trip to the Nationwide to help Nell take out some money and then Argos to get her a festival tent. Pay the £100 annual fee for Banham servicing our burglar alarm. Transfer £2k from my savings to my current account to cover the expenses of the summer.

An encouraging tweet arrives from a fellow writer. Suzie Grogan, a writer and social historian who has previously tweeted to say good things about *Man About Tarn* and also likes both Wordsworth and West Ham (my ideal reader), tweets to say: "Just read your article in the SoA journal. Love it and empathised with it (not the prostate bit, obvs). Hope the subsidence is sorted... I'm working harder than ever for less than ever. But at least we're home to take the parcels in..."

Hmm, perhaps I over-shared a little with the information about my prostate. Following Dr Klopp's zealous internal examination, the most recent scan suggests it is relatively normal-ish for (terrible phrase) a 'man of my age'. I think this a good thing.

Tuesday August 6
We interview a man as a potential lodger. He seems ok and earns a lot of money, but when we do some digging his company seems to work for an arms dealer, so we rule him out. It's tough letting out a room in Ethics. Receive some very useful feedback from Profile Books. They are going to pass on my idea, but have run it past Shaun Bythell's editor who comments:

"Shaun, we think, has an unfair advantage in that he 'runs' a second-hand bookshop. This is a bit like doing up a place in Provence or Andalucía, or setting up a restaurant – one of those dreams people like to buy into, even though the reality is generally a disaster. Being a freelance writer is, well, a bit less of a dream. I know, I

know – I'm part of that world, too. The bookshop locale also helps bring in a cast of characters and some amusing set pieces, and a couple of other voices. That's a tougher call in the freelance writer scenario. So, to make this work, you really will have to dazzle the readers with charm, wit and fun – largely at your own expense. I don't think that's impossible (Spaced didn't have an enormous hinterland) but it's quite a challenge, and I don't think you're there yet with this draft. Hope this is vaguely helpful. Good luck if you decide to run with it."

It's a rejection, but there's something to work on there. Nell leaves for the Boardmasters festival in Cornwall festival in the evening. She rings us at 10.30pm to say it's been cancelled due to predicted high winds, but she and Ruth are still getting the night coach to Penzance. It's a good decision, as she and her friends end up staying in Penzance youth hostel and having their own teenage festival eating croissants, drinking the beer and vodka they had been planning on sneaking into the festival, and making their own entertainment.

Wednesday August 7
Still entertaining my sister. First a trip to Rainham Marshes to walk across the duck boards observing frogs in the liminal marshes and admire the Thames from a surprisingly unspoilt shoreline, then (expensive) dinner at an Italian restaurant with Pam and younger sister Kaz in West Horndon.

Thursday August 8
A trip with Pam to Colchester. While researching my book *The Joy of Essex* I discovered just how much the town had to offer. We look round the castle and the foundations that were part of the Roman temple sacked by Boudicca, then admire the Balkerne Gate, which has

the best Roman arch in Britain and visit the FirstSite art gallery. We also discover the imposing ruins of the abbey by the Colchester Town station. It's a place that should be visited by a lot more tourists, but sadly gets overlooked because it's in Essex and people think it's all *Towie* and fake tan (though the Romans might also have been orange and liked a bit of bling).

Friday August 9

Complete the last of my music biographies on Spanish classical guitarist Alberto Ponce. Can't think why he never made it big in England... Do a blog on how West Ham have fared on transfer deadline deadline day and then a post for my Essex blog (I started it as a promotional tool for my book and still maintain it) about the joys of Colchester. Might as well put my trips with Pam to some use writing-wise. The combined blogs have made 1p on AdSense today.

Apply for a new NUJ press card — at least I'll look like a journalist with it in my wallet. My Over-60 Oyster card arrives three days before my birthday. This will be a massive help. Through being an old git I get free travel on tubes and buses all over London. Rejoice!

Go to see the film *Blinded by the Light* in Walthamstow with Nicola, Pam and our friend Paula. It's the story of an Asian kid in Luton who grows up loving Bruce Springsteen. They've made it a bit Hollywood at times, but it's a good story and as the writer of a few memoirs myself, I resolve to buy Sarfraz Manzoor's book *Greetings From Bury Park* and see what I can learn from it.

Saturday August 10

The opening day of the season sees me at West Ham versus Manchester City with my pals Matt, Michael,

Nigel and Fraser, plus daughter Lola and her Man City-supporting friend Catherine. It doesn't go quite to plan as the Hammers lose 5-0 at home. Things can only get better.

Monday August 12
Still showing my sisters the sights of Essex and places Pam might remember from our childhood. Today we go to Leigh-on-Sea with its delightful old fishing harbour and walk on past the Thames Estuary into Southend. There's big rain though and we end up sheltering in a tea room.

Tuesday August 13
It's my 60th birthday. I didn't want to make a big deal of it, as I've never enjoyed parties where I'm the centre of attention. As a writer/hack I'm much more of an observer rather than a performer. Normally on my birthday I'd be reflecting on the top of a Lake District mountain. But dinner is booked for the evening and Nicola does a good job explaining to my sisters that I like to do a solo walk on my birthday as a treat. Instead of the Lake District I'm trekking from Hackney Wick to Canning Town along the River Lea. And for the first time I use my Over-60 Oyster card to get there for free on the Overground.

Following the Lee Navigation from White Post Lane at Hackney Wick, I soon find myself in the surprisingly leafy and peaceful environs beneath the London Stadium. It's a fine sunny day for solo walking. Leaving the stadium behind it's on past the twin locks of Old Ford Lock and the lock-keeper's cottages that were converted into the *Big Brother* house. One link with West Ham is the site of the converted Percy Dalton's peanut factory — as famously sold on the North Bank.

After going under several large roads in Stratford the

river takes me to the historic Three Mills with its working waterwheels. It was built in 1776 and is the world's largest tidal mill. Then it's on down Bow Creek with fine views of Canary Wharf. I arrive at Cody Dock, which now has a cafe and number of workspaces — though the silted-up old dock reveals how important the River Lea once was as an industrial shipway. Sadly the riverside path is closed beyond the dock, but an alternative route takes the pedestrian down a *Sweeney*-esque road of scrap-metal merchants and back to the Lea at Canning Town.

Bow Creek Ecology Park is an oasis of green opposite the new multi-coloured tower blocks of City Island. The walk ends at East India Dock and then Trinity Buoy Wharf, once used for testing buoys and lighthouses. There's the old lighthouse still there and a cafe with a black taxi deposited on the roof. Across the Leamouth lies the site of Thames Ironworks, now a metal company. West Ham started life here as the Ironworks' works team. Strangely, this being hipster land, there's also a boat with giant orange mushrooms sprouting from its roof. It's a walk that takes in West Ham's current home and the site of the place where it all began. And on a hot day it's all rather beautiful, in a post-industrial kind of way.

By 4.30 I'm back at home and find my family have been touchingly preparing presents. Kaz has arrived with some boxed Punk IPA and a CD, Pam has given me a box of craft beer and *Brilliant, Brilliant, Brilliant Brilliant Brilliant* by Joel Golby. Lola has got me a book on *Literary Wonderlands*, and Nicola has given me a series of outings on the 13th of every month. Nicola, Lola and Nell are busy making a cake. We all end up at Rasa in Stoke Newington and it's a quiet but satisfying evening. The vegetarian curries are great and Nicola persuades everyone to make a little speech and they all say some moving things.

Sixty years. Was it really forty years ago that I was graduating? Was it twenty-one years ago that I became a dad? I'm lucky, I've got married, had children, bought a house, survived the death of my parents, seen West Ham win the Cup twice, travelled to a few countries, been treasurer of Drayton Park School PTA, appeared in the *Guardian* and published 15 books. No-one has asked me to fight in a war. The last few years might have been difficult financially, but I'm lucky in every other way.

Wednesday August 14
Back to work. Sixtieth birthday done. I'm pleased it's over and my 61st birthday will be less of a milestone. Send off my tax return for 2018-19. This year things have improved with the music biographies, more sales of *Man About Tarn* and selling a couple of features. But in the last financial year my turnover is only £2700. After deducting business expenses (stationery, computers, postage, research, etc) my profit is only £450, which isn't going to trouble the taxman too much. It's good for my morale to make a small profit, even if claiming for all my legitimate tax expenses might give me a negative income. If I'm honest, I'm operating at a loss and should probably be claiming universal credit, though hopefully 2019-20 will be a better year. Pride is a funny thing, and at least I've not had to take that job in the off-licence yet — even though I'm sure the purveyors of beers and spirits are very fine people.

Have a coffee while buying Hippy Bread at Salt the Radish café. Tamsin, the friendly barista behind the counter asks me how my writing is going. I don't explain my idea very well saying that I'm working on a writer's diary. I should have said it was a satire on the gig economy. But at least writing still seems glamorous to the cappuccino crowd.

Pam asks me what I do when I don't have any work. I explain that you can always work a full day even if no one is paying you, trying to think up ideas, reading papers and magazines, generally doing more searching than Kevin Rowland did for the young soul rebels. She looks impressed.

In the evening we interview Tom, a potential lodger who commutes to London from France. He has decent social skills and likes the finest wines known to humanity, having worked in the industry, and is a rugby fan (liking any sport is good, even if it's not football) so we think he'll do.

Thursday August 15
Nell's A level results. She has three As! Quite an achievement, and much better than my A level grades. The world is her lobster. After a celebratory breakfast it's off to meet Pilates studio owner Bill and his designer Jim, who is also a playwright. We discuss the newsletter. It seems mainly a case of going through the media for Pilates references and writing some diary-type pieces on them, plus the odd interview with a Pilates teacher. Having once edited the Sidelines column in *Time Out* for nine years and done a weekly column in *Midweek* for a decade I should be able to do that. It will be an interesting monthly retainer.

Home to do some of my weekly music biographies. Nell goes out to celebrate with her fellow sixth-formers and we give a hopeful lecture about not getting drunk. Then read *Berlin 1936: Sixteen Days in August* by Oliver Hilmes, the chosen tome for my sports book group.

Friday August 16
There's a place near us known as 'the elephant house' because it's got a hedge carved in the shape of a series of

elephants thanks to some skilled topiary by the aptly-named Tim Bushe. Only recently it's become something of a crack den and the police are attempting to close it down. Now a local vigilante has driven a car into the hedge, knocking over the walls and destroying half an elephant. The incident has made the local paper.

After surveying the hedge damage I return to upload my last music biography for the week. Then go to the Museum of London with Pam and look at some good displays on deposits in the Thames, though I'm rather museum-ed out by this stage. Nicola returns from paddle boarding in the canal, Lola comes over from Turnpike Lane and Nell stays in for a farewell dinner for Auntie Pam, until 10pm when she heads out.

Saturday August 17
Go with Pam and her suitcase, which is the size of a house to Heathrow. Kaz joins us with her partner Del and we bid farewell over a final meal. It's been good to see her, though after nearly four weeks of entertaining I now need to get back to some work.

Monday August 19
Nicola is still doggedly trying to fill up our rooms and now wants to acquire a Swiss student. Through friends on the same scheme, we have discovered that putting up a Swiss student can earn you a stonking £7k a year for being a surrogate parent. Even I'm a bit tempted. We have a productive meeting with a man called Rick about a potential 17-year-old sixth-form student whose father wants to remove her from her current accommodation. Though later in the week he says that she's staying where she is and we are put back on the waiting list.

Tuesday August 20

Nell arrives home at 4.30am, rather later than her midnight curfew. She has been celebrating for four days now in a sustained bout of hedonism worthy of Billy Idol. Clear up a KFC container and ripped plastic bag from the garden due to the fox. A tax rebate of £475 arrives which is tremendously useful. Do an Essex blog post. I have made 38p on AdSense today, but it's taking forever to reach the £60 Blogger threshold. Sold five copies of *Man About Tarn* over the last week. It's like an old friend that keeps giving, an inadvertent slow-burning half-decent seller.

Do a biography on Singapore national treasure Kit Chan. But amid the bubblegum occasionally someone is really good, like singer Lindsay Ell who has a great voice and is a fine guitarist. Though not *Doobie Dam Dam* by Baneroo, which is the most infernally catchy bubblegum single of all time. I wish I'd never played it, as I can't stop humming it. Still, thanks to the biogs at £10 an entry my turnover was £3139 for the first third of the year — already more than in the whole of 2018-19. Write a list in my notebook of things I must do, like try to find a way back into the *Guardian*. I'm not sure life-coach Karen would approve of this.

Wednesday August 21
Nell went out for a coffee at 2pm with Orla and came back at 3.30am. "Dad, relax, it's summer!" is her defiant text. Hoover outside Nell's bedroom at 10.20am in a bid to try and get her to wake up and keep earlier hours.

My KDP account tells me that 13 yen is coming from Japan for *Man About Tarn* — this sounds exciting until I discover that this is about ten pence. Then there's a duster salesman at the door. "Before you set the dog on me can I ask you to buy one of these household items for the homeless…"

"Sorry we haven't got much money at the moment," I declare, refraining from telling him about the median income of writers. 'Thank you so much, have a good day!"

Start to write up my last Lake District trip as a potential sample book chapter. There must be a sequel in my Lakes adventures somewhere. So many of my recent books have been written without a publisher, simply through a determination not to be excluded. It's a matter of pride that I did eventually find publishers *for The Joy of Essex, Goodbye to Boleyn* and *Man About Tarn*. It would have been very easy to take no as an answer.

Thursday August 22
Do more biogs. Seven this week, lots of J-pop and K-pop. An NHS Bowel cancer detection kit arrives with a mysterious plastic tray and a specimen tube. Apparently I have to catch a poo and stuff a sample into a test tube. How great to be 60.

Saturday August 24
Go to see the exhibition of Olafur Eliasson and Natalia Goncharova at the Tate with Nicola in the members' early hour viewing and have a hearty breakfast after in a nearby cafe. In the evening we go to see *The Weather Man,* a play on sex trafficking at the Park Theatre, which is good but depressing. West Ham win at Watford, which is unexpected.

Sunday August 25
Supping lesson from Nicola. I'm not too bad on my knees, but when I stand up I fall in the canal twice. She's reassuringly calm and coaxes me back on to the board. Luckily I have a buoyancy aid and am attached by a lead to the paddleboard. Though on the bottom I can feel

strange objects, shopping trolleys, safes, maybe discarded manuscripts. I scramble back on board covered in green algae and probably bits of dead eel. She says I should try 60 new things now I'm 60. One is enough, I surmise, though I do manage to stand for ten seconds with Nicola's board parallel to my own to stop it tipping over. My body is as supple as a plank of wood. Best leave this to the hipsters.

Monday August 26
The hottest August bank holiday in years. Do two items for the new Pilates newsletter and learn about scoliosis. Nell is now back from the Victorious festival in Portsmouth. At dinner Nell and myself debate Nicola's apple and cheese pie, trying to decide whether it's a main course or a pudding. "It's like your marmalade that's a drink," says Nell. "My parents didn't like my experimental cooking either," complains Nicola. "They didn't like salads with added bits. You'll see! I'm ahead of my time. In 20 years this will be normal."

Tuesday August 27
Very hot again. My list of music biographies is late arriving. Clear up a mangled polystyrene cup from the garden and also a key left by the fox and a chewed wallet. Nicola is depressed after a university course meeting and thinks she might lose her job next year. We go through the children's books that have been lying for years in a suitcase in our bedroom and decide that we just can't give away the precious story books from our daughters' childhood. Go to the pub with my pal Matt to watch West Ham win at Newport in the League Cup.

Wednesday August 28
A note about *Goodbye to Boleyn* arrives via my website

email. Writers live on these little interactions and it makes the effort of completing a book worth every sweated comma and semi-colon. It reads: "*Hi Pete, I am just like yourself a long-suffering West Ham United supporter. I'm going to be totally honest with you I don't read any books at all in fact I don't read any books and that I have probably read two since I have left school (I'm now 37 years old) but decided that I wanted to read something whilst relaxing next to the pool on our family holiday in northern Cyprus. I chose your book Goodbye to Boleyn and I have just finished it (still sitting next to the pool), I absolutely loved it, it brought back so many memories of Upton Park, where I used to drink, eat, meet friends and the sights and smells of the old place. Reliving those memorable games in that last season as well, I also had a season ticket in the East Stand or Chicken Run, as I liked to call it, I was in the corner right next to the away fans (3rd row back 2nd seat in to be precise). Anyway I have gone off topic, I just wanted to thank you for a great read on my holiday and for the great insight into your love for the club and your story of becoming a West Ham fan, congratulations on such a great book. Come on you Irons! David Harper*"

Friday August 30
Five music biographies finished. KDP reveals that I've sold 11 paperbacks and six e-books of *Man About Tarn* this month, earning £40.79 in royalties. Spend much of the day packing my Gore-Tex gear, walking sticks, boots, map case, Wainwright guides and survival bag, plus a dog bed, as we are finally having our week's family holiday in the Lake District. Who needs the Alps? We are going to Keswick

SEPTEMBER

THINGS CAN ONLY GET WETTER — KEEP TAKING THE PILATES — PARTY TIME — A MAN OF SUBSIDENCE — PAYING GUESTS — SODDEN HANDBAGS — SHE'S LEAVING HOME

Sunday September 1 — Friday September 6

We're in the mainly rainy Lake District for our long-awaited holiday in Keswick. It's good to have the gang back together. It's Nell's last family holiday before she goes to York University. We're joined by big sister Lola and her friend Katy, along with Nicola, Vulcan and myself.

Despite struggling for work all year, whenever the freelancer goes away calls come in. While I'm up Causey Pike, Bill from the Pilates studio rings wanting to bring the first newsletter forward. I explain I'm away without a laptop but can start work on Sunday when I return.

Last summer when we were in Keswick the *Guardian* phoned, incredibly enough, and I was asked to write a short piece on climbing Fleetwith Pike. It seems the only way to guarantee work is to go on holiday. I remember 20 years ago coming down off Coniston Old Man and dealing with some copy changes for a top ten of footballers behaving badly for the *Observer Sport Monthly*. Still, it makes me feel vaguely impressive to be contacted on holiday.

The poor weather can't stop us enjoying our stay, even while Parliament descends into rancour and procedural deadlock over Brexit. After climbing a windswept Sale Fell, Nell and Nicola fall in love with the old prints and rich patina of polish on oak walls of the bar at the

Pheasant Hotel. Me less so, when I learn that a pot of tea and half a pint of beer costs £7.80. Then we wait for a bus in a stone bus shelter at Dubwath, as the heaviest rain we've ever seen bounces up off the tarmac.

Five new Wainwrights are bagged during our stay. Lola and Katy ride electric bikes almost all the way to Buttermere. We all visit the Lakeside theatre to see *Uncle Vanya* updated for the Lake District.

We enjoy a day trip down Honister Slate Mine and then an unexpected walk, in a rare moment of good weather, down Honister Pass and on to Seatoller, where the girls discover an ancient device known as a red telephone box and are so excited they ring Granny Fiona from it.

On another walk I show Nicola the lovely Watendlath Tarn, thinking more about another Lake District book. When a walker tells us a path is a "bit technical" we decide that whatever I write needs a few buzzwords in the title. My walking will have to be extreme or wild and promote wellness.

Saturday Sept 7 — Sunday Sept 8
Return to London and get down to my first Pilates newsletter. There's a short intro from Pete the studio manager and then, thanks to some help from researcher Vicky-Louise, I've written a series of news items on Colin Thackery, the 89-year-old Chelsea pensioner who won *Britain's Got Talent* and does Pilates; Gemma Atkinson from *Emmerdale* beating the baby blues with Pilates; the fact England's World Cup-winning wicket keeper Jos Buttler is married to a Pilates teacher; and there's a farm in Devon offering Pilates with pigs. I don't get a byline, but I'm charging £150 a day (the rates for writing and subbing days don't seem to have changed for a decade) and it's going to help to have a regular gig each

month. Maybe I like Pilates…

Monday September 9
The fox has left a mangled single converse trainer in the garden to welcome us home. Read the final pages of *Warlight* by Michael Ondaatje for the book group tomorrow. List the invites sent out for our forthcoming party to celebrate my 60th, Nell's 18th and Lola's 21st at the Brownswood pub.

Tom the new lodger moves in. He is commuting from Toulouse and has an early night after getting up at 4am to fly to London. He seems convivial though, and arrives with a bottle of wine, which is promising.

Tuesday September 10
Pick up a lacerated Burger King coffee cup by the French windows. Do my first music biography of the week. Walk down Seven Sisters Road to get an £8 haircut. Incredibly, after half a year's blogging, AdSense on my Blogger account is now just £2.87 away from making the £60 threshold. Book group at Dorothy's house in the evening. The usual mix of nibbles, wine and gossip with a spot of literature added in.

Wednesday September 11
Walk Vulcan and stop for a coffee in the Park theatre. Race through the final four music biographies of the week. That's £40 bagged for the day. And here's something… It's not often I'm on the same page as Vladimir Lenin, Andrea Levy, Louis MacNeice and John Stuart Mill. Islington Council publishes a magazine called *Islington Life* and I've made it into their 'literary road map of Islington', celebrating the borough's authors, poets, screenwriters and playwrights. It lists me as, "the author of *West Ham: Irons in the Soul* and other titles."

We're woken up at 11pm by a text, and have to put an extra mattress in the guest room for Nell's guests who are coming back from the pub.

Thursday September 12
Send a *Doctor Who* idea to the *New Statesman* and the *Guardian's* Short Cuts column. It's on how the Doctor would stop a no-deal Brexit by perhaps discovering that Boris is in fact a giant Teselecta robot crewed by tiny Brexiteers, or imbuing Angela 'Donna' Rayner with Time Lord knowledge to dismantle the reality bomb, thereby removing Planet UK from its pocket universe, or maybe unmasking Jacob Rees-Mogg as the Master's latest cunning disguise — hence the insolent lolling in Parliament and aversion to changing nappies of small humans. Or using the restoration field of the Pandorica to collide with the exploding Tardis and create an invisible border somewhere near the Irish backstop.

At 12.30pm I enter the kitchen for lunch to discover two teenage boys making fried eggs with Nell for a late breakfast. They are the survivors of last night's late-arriving sleepover.

In the evening it's my sport book group with Peter, Tony C and Tony. We sit at a table outside Franco Manca at Russell Square and discuss *Berlin 1936: 16 Days in August* by Oliver Hilmes. It's a brilliant book on the Nazi Olympics and looks at the human stories of the people living in Berlin as Hitler sportwashed his regime. Hilmes really gets over the lavish hospitality and massive parties the regime gave for journalists. Would we have been there enjoying the free beer and canapés or investigating the truth behind the façade? There must have been freelancers there who just wanted a free meal and all the booze they could drink.

Friday September 13
Work on my speech for our combined birthday parties on
Saturday. And what about this? I have passed the £60
AdSense threshold! Someone in Switzerland has clicked
on £2.34 of adverts today. It's taken all year but I've got
there. One small click for man, one giant click for my
bank balance.

Go to Leather Lane to research some falafel street
food for a feature Nicola is doing. Any excuse for a wrap.
Nell's friend Elsa arrives from Wales to stay for the
weekend. The Virgin modem suddenly expires for no
good reason.

Saturday September 14
It's our big party at the Brownswood pub. I arrive early
with Nicola and have the usual panic that no-one will
come. We've put £250 behind the bar and the pub say we
need to sell £1000 in drinks. Some of my friends should
drink that in a couple of rounds...

But from 7.30pm guests start to filter in and then it's
packed. It's moving how so many people have turned up.
My old school friends are there, Sarah from Kent, Nick,
Tim and Mark, plus Katie the wife of my late school
friend Paul with new partner Alex and dog Scampy.
There's all the old parents from Drayton Park primary
school, Julie and Ben from Winsley near Bath, my old
friend Julia from Cardiff is also there, with whom I used
to flatshare in West Kensington back in 1982. On the
family front there's Nicola's mum with Anthony, plus
brother Drew with Kate and children Rose and Jago. Plus
several of my West Ham friends, the book group and the
Beta Males pub quiz team.

We've put £250 behind the bar. Nicola and myself
have been given a numbered card that we have to quote to
the bar staff to get free drinks, so we spend a lot of time at

the bar ordering drinks for new guests. Nell arrives with a posse of older teenagers who gleefully partake of the free booze. Lola is there with her Turnpike Lane entourage and the finest minds from SOAS. We're enjoying ourselves so much we can hardly take our eyes off the bar tab. After 90 minutes or so we discover that the free beer has already reached £350 and the bar staff have forgotten all about our limit. We tell them to stop before bankruptcy looms and retreat to the upstairs function room.

Lola and Nell stand on a table looking young and glamorous and give an impressive impromptu speech. Then it's my turn to perform, starting with a Brexit joke by revealing it's not actually any of our birthdays today, they have in fact been prorogued to September 14 so there can be no room for discussion — but we will definitely be leaving the pub by the end of September 14 and if not I would rather die in a ditch.

I thank my wife and daughters and my West Ham friends for sticking by me and the Hammers through thin and thin. Then I list some of achievements such as marriage, property-owning after years as a rent boy, becoming a dad, seeing West Ham win the FA Cup twice, being published in the *Guardian*, writing books, and most importantly, having a Wainwright wall-chart and ticking off 146 Lakeland fells so far. Though I've not as yet seen attack ships on fire off the shoulder of Orion, but I might after a few more pints of craft beer.

The rest of the evening passes in a pleasing blur of bonhomie. A drink in the pub is my ideal way to celebrate 60 years, not too formal, just a convivial evening with old friends and family.

At around half past one Nicola and myself stagger home wheeling a shopping trolley full of birthday booty and carrying several bags of stuff on top. There's a crate of beer from Greene King from Mark, single malt whisky from Martin, champagne from Fraser, Hawaiian beer from Sue and Richard, crates of craft beer from unknown persons, plus a cactus from Jackie and a theatre voucher from Andrew and Jo. And the books, the books: *Fire on the Moon* by Norman Mailer from Robert and Sarah, *How to be a Footballer* by Peter Crouch, Iain M Banks, Bill Bryson, *Lonely Planet's Ultimate United Kingdom Travel List*, *Extreme Rambling by Mark Thomas*, Simon Kuper's book on Ajax, *Thirty One Nil* by James Montague, *Notes on a Nervous Planet* by Matt Haig... For some reason people seem to think beer and football books are the key to my heart.

"People seem to really like you..." says my wife as we walk along Brownswood Road, sounding slightly surprised. It's all a bit of an *It's a Wonderful life* moment.

Sunday September 15
Spend the morning opening my presents with Nicola and deciding which beer to drink first. Unexpectedly I'm offered a free ticket to Watford versus Arsenal by Ben Bradman and despite my hangover go to watch an entertaining 2-2 draw. It makes a change not to worry about who wins and even better, I get there for nothing with my new 60+ Oyster card. Travel has suddenly become a hell of a lot cheaper.

Monday September 16
Wait in for the man from Virgin to replace our dead modem. He says our old one was way out of date and we are now back online. Tired after the weekend. Write thank you emails to our party guests while Nicola holds a school governors meeting in her office.

Luciana our second new lodger arrives. Spend some of

the afternoon setting up Lola's old bedroom for her and also Tom's sofa bed in the front room. Like Tom, Luciana lives in France, and comes over via the Eurostar. She's the sort of lodger who likes to stay and leave early in the morning with a minimum of fuss, which suits us. Two lodgers both paying £30 a night for two to three nights a week will help greatly with finances.

It's the Pub Quiz in the evening, with my thoughts being distracted by Aston Villa versus West Ham on the pub TV. The Beta Males come a disappointing sixth.

Tuesday September 17
Cut the garden hedge (which is across two street fronts as we're a corner house and extends roughly the length of the Great Wall of China) so it looks well-groomed for the subsidence meeting at our house tomorrow. Walk the dog. Compile two music biographies. Watch the *Doctor Who* story *Turn Left* in the evening, where Donna has to choose between two different life paths. Was there a turn left moment in my life? Perhaps in one life there was no subsidence.

Wednesday September 18
A subsidence meeting takes place at our house. Our structural engineer Martin knows the insurer's structural engineer Kevin. They do a bit of engineer-type rutting over cracks and monitor readings, before agreeing that some vegetation should be removed and our three small apple trees in the front garden will have to go. Nicola looks distraught. Then it will be monitored for a year by Jarndyce and Jarndyce. We dispense coffee and biscuits and try to keep up with the complex data surrounding the fact that our house is falling down.

Thursday September 19

Write biographies of two recently deceased American pop musicians, Daniel Johnston a sensitive songwriter beset by mental health problems but whose deceptively simple songs were covered by the likes of Lana Del Ray and influenced Kurt Cobain; and blue-collar rocker and MTV pioneer Eddie Money. Writing a condensed history of dead rockers takes more time as there's a whole career to summarise, but in many ways these are the more interesting assignments.

Nicola leaves to teach riding at Trent Park, still apparently unfazed by travelling on the Piccadilly line in jodhpurs and a whip. Pick up our organic vegetable bags from the collection point at the reservoir and cook dinner for Nicola when she returns from giving riding lessons.

Friday September 20
Two weeks after its arrival I finally get the courage to collect the NHS-requested poo sample, required in order to detect bowel cancer in the over-60s. Nurse, the screens... Take Vulcan for a walk, write up the Beta Males' match review. Start work on writing up our recent holiday in Keswick for my projected book on walking all the Wainwright fells. These days being a writer is about having the faith to keep going and gamble.

Attend the Green Party quiz night at Islington Ecology Centre with Nicola, Andrew and Jo. We have an enjoyable time and enjoy the vegan curry, but fail to win the prize of a box of chocolates.

Saturday Sept 21
Extinction Rebellion have closed down the Oxford Circus roundabout. Trying, as ever, to make cash from chaos, I give my 2008 book *There's A Hippo in my Cistern* a plug on my Pete May Writer Facebook page with a link to the book on Amazon. The message reads: "Yesterday's

climate change protests make this seem rather relevant today — *Hippo* was about being an eco-worrier back in 2008, when 'woke' was something that applied to your alarm clock..."

Sunday September 22
Take Nell to West Ham versus Manchester United. It's her last game before going to university and astonishingly the Hammers win 2-0 against Ole Gunnar Solskjaer's men. "Dad, you never said this was going to happen," says my puzzled daughter. We retreat to a bar on a boat on the River Lea to celebrate with a pint of bottled Doom Bar. The Irons are in the top six and surely destined for a fine season. What could possibly go wrong?

Monday September 23
Write a match review of the Man United game on my West Ham blog. It's enjoyable to do after a win, but will probably only make a few pence in advertising revenue. But still, through doing a blog I had the material to write about West Ham's last season at the Boleyn Stadium in *Goodbye to Boleyn*, so it's not always a wasted effort and it amuses my pals and a small coterie of loyal readers. Then do my first music biography of the week.

Tuesday September 24
Awake to the whiff of soggy leather. Nicola has been out paddleboarding doing her 'Plastic Patrol' on the canal. She and a group of volunteers pick up all the flotsam on the water and remove it for recycling or the bin. Only now she is drying out 15 wet handbags over the chairs in our kitchen. "I pulled out a bin-liner full of handbags that was at the bottom of the canal," she explains. "Once they're dry I can give them to the charity shop. And there was a pair of jeans as well."

It's all very *Peaky Blinders* and surely hints at nefarious goings-on by the towpath. The handbags have clearly been stolen, as there's nothing in them bar one set of headphones. Or is it Nicola who is actually the handbag thief hiding behind a concocted story of finding them in the canal?

"Mum why are there wet handbags all over the kitchen?" asks Nell.

"It's OK darling, you can have one for university."

There's also a pair of jeans with the handbags that she's retrieved from the murky depths. "Hmm, these jeans might fit me," muses Nicola. I point out that they probably belong to a dead person.

Nell is making her farewells. We travel to Romford on the train to have an all-you-can-eat lunch with Auntie Kaz. Then come back home to listen to a little of Jeremy Corbyn's speech at the Labour Party conference, promising inevitable victory against that chancer Johnson. Finish writing up my sample chapter on Keswick.

Wednesday September 25
A rainy autumnal day, all grey skies and damp wood chips in the chicken run. Made 24p on AdSense today and one digital copy of *Man About Tarn* has sold, netting me £1.72. Read through my *Man About Tarn 2* chapters and try to decide if it has legs. Write two music biogs. Go to see Lola in her café, where she is behind the counter dealing with the Geordie postman's coffee and discussing her next magazine with her flatmate Oscar.

Upstairs Nell is packing her cases and backpack for university. Rather touchingly she is taking a copy of my book *There's a Hippo in my Cistern* for her campus bookshelf.

Thursday September 26

One of Nicola's Islington Faces subjects, Mick Fitzgerald, calls round to collect some memorabilia he loaned to her exhibition. He tells me how much he enjoyed my book on Sunday league football, *Sunday Muddy Sunday* and says he has seen *Goodbye To Boleyn* in Foyles at Stratford.

Nell takes me for a late birthday brunch of poached eggs at the Common Ground cafe. Return home to find Nicola has hung all the sodden handbags on the washing line in our garden, just to get that Artful Dodger effect for the neighbours.

Do a post on Facebook wondering if proroguing Parliament is a violation of the terms of the Shadow Proclamation. Write another two music biographies, earning £20. Nell goes to Franca Manca and the Camden Head for another farewell evening with her numerous friends. There's a belated response to my *Doctor Who* idea from the *Guardian*: "Sorry for the delay in coming back to you. I think I'm going to pass in this instance, as it isn't quite right for G2, but thank you for thinking of us and good luck placing it." Oh well, it's a response at least.

Friday September 27
One of the sodden handbags has fallen from the washing line and been savaged by the fox. I persuade Nicola to take the bags that are semi-dry to the charity shop and wonder if the police will be calling to accuse her of canal-washing the proceeds of crime. Order some author copies of *Man About Tarn* in the hope of making some Christmas sales to friends.

Meet my old 1980s flatmate Sean at Trafalgar Square for a late lunch in the crypt at St Martin's church. He now lives in Cardiff and is thriving as a tax inspector, though I don't suspect he'll be staking out my office just yet as my turnover is unlikely to trouble the Inland Revenue.

Saturday September 28
She's leaving home. We take the train to York with Nell and her three cases and backpack, containing at least 57 coats. We're travelling with Anna, also now a Yorkie and one of Nell's oldest friends from primary school, plus Anna's mum Oxana and her new baby. Nell's bedroom is just like my old room at Lancaster University 42 years ago, while Nicola actually went to York herself so it's especially nostalgic for her. We're shown round by enthusiastic second-years, including Nathan who has ditched chemistry for drama and is now doing a drag act. Nicola introduces Nell to Tom, the boy in the room opposite.

We help our daughter unpack, look at the college bar, say an emotional goodbye to her with a mix of excitement and sadness. She… we gave her most of our lives. Nicola and myself head to the tiny Blue Bell pub and then have dinner at a Chinese restaurant before catching the train back to London, surrounded by stag and hen parties from Doncaster. We have kept Nell safe for 18 years and now she is an adult. She texts to say she has ordered a pizza and is going out to the Freshers' welcome party. We arrive home to a house that seems increasingly empty.

Sunday September 29
Nicola busies herself taking her reclaimed canal handbags to the Crisis charity shop. She's dried out the canal jeans and says they fit. Actually the canal-washed denim looks quite smart, that is if you don't mind wearing a murder victim's jeans. Nicola evidently doesn't.

We take Vulcan along the Parkland Walk to Highgate and back and then watch Jane Austen's *Sanditon* and all sorts of lesbian goings on with Miss Lister in Sally

Wainwright's drama *Gentleman Jack*. "This is our life for the next 25 years," muses Nicola, from our vacated nest. "Yes, watching Sunday evening TV together, it's perfect," I counter.

Monday September 30
Rain all day. "It's the autumn of our lives," I suggest. The tree outside our bedroom window has yellow leaves. Nell's room looks bare. Do my first biography of the week and take comfort with routine. Fiddle with the landline — the office phone appears to be broken. Email the subsidence man as the crack in the living room has got worse.

Nicola is out teaching at university, the riding school and the boat club. Sold two paperbacks of *Man About Tarn* today. This brings the monthly KDP figures up to 10 paperbacks and eight e-books of *Man About Tarn* sold, plus one print version of *Flying So High: West Ham's Cup Finals*, netting a total of £41.45 in royalties.

Our lodgers Tom and Luciana arrive with their suitcases, having both journeyed from France in the morning at some ungodly hour to get to work. Their presence helps to fill the house up. They might both be in their middle years, but they are still going to have to get used to being parented.

OCTOBER

ADSENSE AND SENSIBILITY — BELGIAN IRON — IN PRAISE OF THE NEWHAM BOOKSHOP — EXTINCTION REBELLION — BOLLOCKS TO BREXIT — IN THE GUTTER — ALL THAT JAZZ

Tuesday October 1

The Pilates studio has paid me £150 for my day's work on the first newsletter, which is useful income. At last AdSense have also transferred £62.73 into my bank account — it's taken since July 2018 to reach the £60 threshold, but it's still satisfying to earn something from my blogging. Another £16 has arrived from my old school friend Sarah, who bought two copies of *Man About Tarn* at my party for her nephew Bill — who is apparently my biggest fan, at least according to Sarah.

Look through my accounts. I still like to keep paper accounts in a Collins Cathedral Analysis book with the figures added in pencil. Seeing income written on paper just seems so much more satisfying than on an Excel spreadsheet, not that I have ever mastered those dizzying columns. I'm about to hit £4000 income for the first six months of the tax year, which is good, a big improvement on last year. Though it's still pretty abysmal by the standards of any normal profession.

Nicola has been given two free tickets for the Faber 90th birthday party celebrations at UCL in the evening, where it's stanza room only. We see recordings of Ted Hughes and Sylvia Plath plus live performances from Simon Armitage and several other poets.

Wednesday October 2

A very nice email arrives on my website from a Belgian West Ham fan. It reads: *Dear Mister May, A few years ago I met you at the Newham Bookshop, because Vivian has asked you to sign some of your books for a Belgian Iron from Antwerp. This year on holiday in Italy I was reading your book and to my surprise you mentioned that encounter. What an honour, even more since you called me a university lecturer, which was another first. I'm just a student counsellor at a centre for adult education and I teach in a prison in Antwerp. I'm going to be in Stratford for the game against Norwich. I'd love to thank you in person with a few special beers from Antwerp after or before the game. From what I can gather from your books, you're a bit of a beer lover. If you'd rather just spend your time with your regular group of football enthusiasts, I'd fully understand. Just let me know. Thanks again for mentioning me, that was so special. Kind regards, Ivan Robeyns*

I write back to say that unfortunately I'm going to be in the Lake District for the Norwich game, but thank him for his kind words. It's gratifying to think that somewhere in a prison in Antwerp Ivan might be rehabilitating Belgian recidivists by reading aloud my descriptions of eggs, chips and beans in Ken's Café before a West Ham home defeat.

Thursday October 3

We phone Nell in the morning, which cheers us both up. Seems like she's settling into student life and discovering York's nightclubs. Nicola is editing the latest issue of *the Pavement*. "Do you know it's only £5 for a blow job under Hastings Pier? It used to be £10," she tells me. "It will be down to £2.50 after Brexit," I joke. As many of her writers are former or current homeless people with various addictions, she's discovering many new facts about life on the streets. Should either of us end up beneath Hastings Pier offering such services, we'll know what to charge.

Do a phone interview with Katsura, a Pilates teacher, for the Pilates newsletter, tapping away at my keyboard as she speaks. It's a profile piece for the clients so they know a bit more about the teachers, how they got into Pilates, what they enjoy about teaching and how clients can bring Pilates into their everyday life. Like a lot of users, Katsura started to teach Pilates after it helped her recover from a dance injury. At least I'm using some journalistic skills to write a 500-word profile.

Friday October 4

"Here are my home grown tomatoes!" says Nicola proudly entering the kitchen holding a colander of red and green tomatoes. "You can use these burst tomatoes in the stew tonight — oh, that's a slug." Thank goodness little Nell isn't here, who has spent much of her childhood traumatised by hairs in soup and snails in lettuces.

Complete my music biographies and send them to Jen at the bibliographical data services company. This week it's been Hardy (American country singer, noted for his witty *Rednecker* single), Yumo Matsutoya (J-Pop), Baby Shima (Malaysian pop), The Pink Fairies (old hippy rockers), MKTO (American pop) and Josh Kaufman (American pop). I'm going to be unstoppable at pub quizzes one day.

Saturday October 5

Do an interview with Rosa at the Newham Bookshop. It's always a pleasure to help Vivian and the staff at one of London's best independent bookshops. Rosa is working on the project Writing and Reading Newham, which is recording the history of the Newham Bookshop as a learning resource for local school children. She records my thoughts on doing signings at the Newham Bookshop, what the shop means to West Ham fans, the poetry of my childhood journeys from Upminster along the District line and my thoughts on the qualities needed to become a writer. It's flattering to think that soon my words will be an educational resource for the teachers of Newham.

Following the interview I meet Lola and we go on to the London Stadium to watch West Ham ruin everything by losing 2-1 (rather unluckily) at home to Crystal Palace.

Monday October 7

Annie, a green friend from Wales, comes to stay. She's down for the Extinction Rebellion protests and has previously dressed as a red rebel, one of a group of silent red figures who move slowly through the streets looking mournful for the planet. I explain that I can't go to XR as I have to write a Pilates newsletter — which must be the most Islington-sounding excuse ever.

Woke daughter Lola reveals on WhatsApp that she is not a fan of XR: "Telling you to get arrested because of white privilege is why I dislike them, their understanding of race politics is deeply flawed." Though she does think Nicola's picture of the red rebels in Trafalgar Square is pretty cool.

A nice tweet from a man who likes my *Author* piece. Historical writer Greg Lewis tweets: "Hi Pete, just to say I'm catching up with the Society of Authors mag and loved your diary. Hope KDP is being kind to you!"

Tuesday October 8

"Apparently Finsbury Park is flooding. Are u flooded?" asks Lola on WhatsApp. Then she sends a video of Queen's Drive, a road quite near us, submerged under a foot of water that is now pouring into gardens and basements. Blimey. Our water pressure was down this morning but there's no flooding in our street.

Nicola says the Castle Canoeing Centre is acting as a refuge for flooded locals. I walk across to Queen's Drive to find it sealed off with a river flowing down the road and water board men in high-viz jackets scurrying around in panic. Fink's Cafe has been inundated and so has the Sylvanian Families shop on Brownswood Road, where I spent many happy hours with my daughters selecting very expensive furry families. The Islington tsunami has arrived. I wonder if helicopters will soon be parachuting in emergency supplies of Arabica coffee beans and sourdough.

Return home to find several videos of the tsunami on Facebook, along with many similar jokes. But a good writer has to work despite natural disasters. I write a West Ham blog post and work on my Pilates newsletter. This month there's *Strictly Come Dancing's* Karen Hauer praising Pilates in the *Telegraph*, Emma Watson being snapped at her Pilates studio by the *Daily Mail*, and a piece on Pilates and flexibility in the *Times*.

In the afternoon I head down to Trafalgar Square to have a look at the Extinction Rebellion protests. Trafalgar Square has been taken over by tents and volunteers are handing out stews. Along Whitehall there are sound systems, dancing and more people camping in tents. Boris Johnson has labelled the XR lot "uncooperative crusties", but I wonder if they might just all be dreadlocked authors waiting for a KDP payment to come through.

XR is certainly raising awareness about the huge danger the world is in, though with its zeal for getting arrested there's also something a little too cultish about it for my liking. Rightly or wrongly, writers tend to be observers rather than activists, and my fears are confirmed when a splinter group stop commuter trains at Canning Town a few days later. The message has to be clear to keep the public onside and it's hard to explain climate change to people who are trying to punch you because they don't get paid if they don't get to their gig economy jobs. But still, for all the movement's faults, at least they are trying to do something while the world burns. As the rain suddenly cascades down I retreat into Waterstone's and buy a novel. Then return home to do another music biography before bed.

Wednesday October 9
Complete another eclectic set of music biographies; Canada country singer MacKenzie Porter, American Jazz fusion artist Bobbi Humphrey, Brazilian *bossa nova* star Wendy Sa and American soul/jazz artist Baby Face Willette. Then look at the online premiere of *Mission to the Unknown*, a missing *Doctor Who* episode now recreated by actors in authentic black and white at the University of Central Lancashire. One for the Whovians like me, complete with Daleks and plastic jungles, and all thoroughly enjoyable.

Friday October 11
Go downstairs to let Vulcan out and discover two foxes asleep on top of the chicken coop. Might it be possible to negotiate some kind of Good Friday Agreement between the foxes and chickens? As one of them looks like a large dog fox and a bit of a bruiser I take Vulcan out of the front door to attend to his ablutions. Nicola comes downstairs to look at the foxes. "Ah, they're asleep, do leave them there." I'm not sure the chickens feel the same way. I go outside to take a photo and the foxes look back at me like teenagers on a sleepover. They are resting and not going to move just yet for some uncool old human.

The morning is an uneasy stand-off until the foxes eventually slink away.

Saturday October 12
Awake to dimly recall a dream about meeting a publisher, though I can't remember how it went. Nicola says I should look it up in her book *A Dictionary of Dreams* by Gustavus Hindman Miller. It was published in 1909, just ten years after Freud's *The Interpretation of Dreams,* and bizarrely it has a section on publishers appearing in dreams: "To dream of a publisher foretells long journeys and aspirations to the literary craft," it begins, rather obviously. "For a publisher to reject your manuscript denotes that you will suffer disappointment at the miscarriage of cherished designs. If he accepts it, you will rejoice in the full fruition of your hopes. If he loses it, you will suffer evil at the hands of strangers."

Never mind the casual sexism of assuming that all publishers are men, I should perhaps just be grateful that no publisher, real or dreamed, has ever lost my manuscript. These days it's much easier to simply drag an email to the Trash basket.

Monday October 14
Stagger downstairs to make Nicola a cup of coffee and a cup of boiled water, feeling fatigued as I often do in the mornings before my caffeine fix. Let Vulcan out into the back garden only for an almighty kerfuffle to break out as Vulcan races for the hedge and round to the side of the chicken coop. Sitting on the roof of the chicken coop is a young fox, looking very calm and terrorising chickens Margaret Hatcher and Egg Miliband. We've been too soft on foxes. I'm worried Vulcan might get hurt if he gets to fight the fox, so with my dressing gown flapping in the wind and possibly exposing myself, I lunge at the fox

with a mop. Luckily Nicola doesn't know what's going on. Years of watching hooligan football firms in action pay off, as after several mop lunges the fox ambles off into next door's garden, leaving it's sharp odour behind. Vulcan growls at the fence.

Chickens sorted I feed Vulcan his dog food and collect the milk from the doorstep. Only one of the empty bottles has been kicked over and has left shattered glass all over our doorstep. Was this the work of the fox too? I get the brush and dustpan and marvel at how many pieces of sharp glass can result from one shattered bottle. Then I notice that next door's cat has been sick on our garden path. Delightful. I'm not touching it.

Return to the kitchen to put the coffee on just as the sound of piercing cutting starts up from next door's garden. Trista and Andrew's artist pal Jules is making a set of bunk beds for their girls, which involves a lot of electric sawing of plywood. It's not going to be a peaceful morning. Take our coffees and Nicola's water up to the bedroom and slump into bed again. *Today* is on the radio alarm broadcasting with interminable Brexit items. Perhaps I should just go back to sleep.

Receive a round-robin email from Karen the life-coach, who must be inundated with clients at present. She talks about breathing during breaks, writing down positive things, looking at nature for at least 12 seconds and being aware of negative thoughts. It concludes with: "Wishing you well and the daily practice of enjoying and noticing things — beauty and judgements!" Decide to notice my chickens more and rid myself of all negative thoughts concerning foxes.

Tuesday October 15
It's time to tackle the box of toys that has been in our bedroom for several years. We put away childish things

when our youngest daughter started to appreciate Zoella and teenage beauty tips more than Silly Bandz. I'm making slow progress with the box. Barbie dresses and jeans lie here, plus lots of Sylvanian Families figures and their fixtures and fittings, such as miniature pizzas, egg slices, sideboards and a portrait of the extended badger family. The girls loved these animal figures so much that we can't contemplate throwing any of them away.

A broken clockwork shark, half a plastic recorder and a few useless pens have been placed in the bin after half an hour. But I'm not keen on losing the monster finger puppets. The David Tennant-era *Doctor Who* stickers bring back lots of happy memories and have been removed to my sock drawer. Perhaps the diplodocus model might be good for possible grandchildren. Parenthood seems to both last forever and be gone in the time it takes to dress a Barbie. One day we may be buried in our bedroom by an avalanche of juvenile ephemera. Future archaeologists will conclude we lived in some kind of plastic cargo cult.

And now Nicola says I've been clearing out the wrong box. This is only Box Number One that has induced intimations of mortality. It's Box Number Two that has the really serious kiddie clutter in it.

Wednesday October 16
Write a couple of music biographies and then go to Westbourne Park for lunch with Jonathan, a housing campaigner whom I know from the 1980s, when I lived in a tower block on the Walterton and Elgin estate in west London. It's all a bit mysterious. He's campaigning to get another estate run by the tenants, which is a good news story, although already covered in quite a few papers. There might be a book in it he thinks but he doesn't seem to have a publisher or any money on offer. I'm not sure

I'm the right man to write it either, as I'm not a housing journalist and it would probably involve trawling through 30 years of council meeting minutes.

I think maybe he's seen a few of my pieces in the *Guardian* and assumes I can get a book deal instantly, without realising how difficult the market is. To write a book you have to be massively enthusiastic about it and it doesn't quite feel like my kind of project. He does buy me a veggie chilli for lunch, which is good of him. I leave still a little unsure what he's proposing.

Thursday October 17
A rush to finish the week's music biographies. This week it's been American jazz artists Blue Mitchell and the Bill Charlap Trio, French hippy rapper Kikesa, K-pop singer Jvcki Wai (yes she does spell it like that) and US country act Love and Theft.

Friday October 18
Walk Vulcan and then have a coffee with my neighbour Nicolette, also a writer and journalist. I mention that I'm doing a talk next week for £30 expenses and she tells me about all the events she's asked to chair for next-to-nothing. We have an enjoyable chat bemoaning our lack of remuneration. Go back home to work on preparing my Power Point presentation on the Lake District for next week's talk at the Stuart Low Trust.

Saturday October 19
A busy day. Watch West Ham lose at Everton with my pal Fraser in the Mabel pub near Euston station. Then move on to the anti-Brexit march to Parliament, where we bump into the journalist Rosie Millard, for whom we once dog-sat. I'm not sure it will change anything but it feels good to be out with a million like-minded people

and to walk next to a giant model of Dominic Cummings with devil-ears and what seems to be a huge phallus attached to an effigy of Boris Johnson. Then it's on to a post-demo pub drink with my old friends Katie, Lindsey and Sue and then dinner with Nicola at Denis and Clare's house. Denis is a proper, albeit overworked journalist, being the health editor of the *Guardian* and also a perpetually frustrated West Ham fan, which is not very good for his health.

Monday October 21
Hoover the rooms ready for the lodgers to arrive, clear the extension of dog hairs and dust, give the downstairs bathroom a quick scrub. I'm not sure if Leo Tolstoy ever had to prepare rooms for paying guests, though if he had it might have helped him cut down on his description of the Battle of Borodino. Send an email to housing activist Jonathan explaining that I'm perhaps not the man to do whatever he wants me to do, though I'll keep an eye on what's happening with his campaign. Start the week's music biographies.

Tuesday October 22-Wednesday October 23
A long-standing trip arranged to visit to Bristol to see my old flat-mate John. From Bristol we drive to Cardiff where he's booked tickets to see the Welsh-speaking band 9Bach. The price of a round is pleasingly cheap and 9Bach intone in Welsh before images of mountains and it's all very atmospheric and Celtic, even if I don't understand a word. The next morning we explore the docks of the Avon and surprisingly I bump into my near-neighbour Mike's son Callum, who is now taking a boat-building course in Bristol. That sounds like a proper job compared to sanding down words and trying to plug leaky prose.

Thursday October 24

The fox has left a ripped Lidl bag by French windows and several pieces of lacerated silver foil. I deal with the man who has come to give the boiler its annual service, which costs another £100. More music biographies to do. Today it's Gary Glitter, about whom I know a great deal. He's in the news because his single *Rock & Roll Part 2* features in the movie *The Joker*. The man might have proved to be a monster, but the glam rock he produced was certainly memorable. And I still like Joan Jett's cover of *Do You Wanna Touch Me?* which I just played on YouTube. My work is completed by a Christian rock group, a country singer and a couple of Latin acts and it's £50 in the bag to go towards my half of the boiler service fee.

Friday, October 25

"This is terrible! They're cutting down my apple trees!" moans a tearful Nicola. The insurers have finally moved into action and are cutting down the three apple trees that Nicola planted in our front garden some years ago in the hope of curing our subsidence.

"We might finally get something done about the house now... and they can leave the logs as firewood."

"But it's nature! What about the birds? It's our *Silent Spring...*"

"At least it's lighter in the kitchen now. And those tree surgeons are only doing their job."

"That's what the Nazis said, they're tree Nazis!"

"Well, we'd still better offer them a coffee..."

After the tree murderers have done their job they give us a survey to fill in about how well they have done their job.

After the deforestation of our garden I finish off preparing my talk on the Lake District for the Stuart Low

Trust. The Trust helps people with mental health and social isolation issues. I've previously given a talk there on my book *The Joy of Essex*.

Arriving at 7pm I'm a little nervous, but everyone is very hospitable and first there's the communal meal of tea and a sandwich followed by some oranges. Nicola has cycled up from her lecturing at Elephant and Castle to come and hear my talk, having partially recovered from the tree-felling of the morning.

My first gambit is to show them my backpack, survival bag and waterproofs. There's a nice big screen and once I get going on the Power Point presentation my confidence returns. Writers love talking about their own work and they have foolishly given me a microphone. I click through pictures of my book cover, the main Lakes, the covers of Alfred Wainwright's pictorial guides, Stickle Tarn, my daughters on Gowbarrow Fell, and the Wasdale Head Inn and the Mortal Man pub.

After exploring the main themes of *Man About Tarn* and reading out some extracts the crowd of 50 or so people prove very enthusiastic at asking questions, even if there is a long digression on the clocks going back this weekend. There are a lot of questions on what sandwiches you can get there and where you can stay. One man actually remembers seeing Alfred Wainwright filming with the BBC at Dent.

A few members of the Trust ask to have their photos taken with me and surprisingly some of the more affluent users buy three copies of my books. Then it's time to leave for a quick pint in the King's Head with Nicola, feeling like the Alfred Wainwright of Upper Street. It might only be £30 in expenses and three books sold netting another £24, but the evening helps a very worthwhile charity and makes me feel appreciated. I've never spoken in public about the Lakes before and it seems like a memorable first. For years I was an amateur plodder up mountains and now I'm an expert, at least in N1.

Saturday October 26
Watch West Ham draw 1-1 with Sheffield United then race over to the White Bear at Oval to see my Hammers pal Michael the Whovian's play *Maggie and Ted.* He's managed to get together a group of fine actors to perform it and the arguments over Europe seem rather pertinent to Brexit Britain. Michael has written books on Nicholas 'The Brigadier' Courtney, Ted Heath and gay Tories but is now pursuing his dream with his third play. Though as with writing, success depends on a combination of determination, finances, fashion, contacts and luck.

Sunday October 27
Walk part of the Thames Path on a crisp autumnal day. Nicola has come up with a list of long-distance walking projects to get over empty nest syndrome. With Vulcan we trek from Windsor to Maidenhead, which is 14 miles or so, meandering with the river beneath overhanging trees and eventually catching a glimpse of the grand estate of Cliveden, where the Profumo affair took place. We enjoy a very welcome coffee in Café Nero after a long walk to Maidenhead station and sleep well after a restorative beer at home.

Monday October 28
A man comes to look at our gutters — though I am looking at the stars. Having agreed to repair a couple of leaks for £85, Kevin the roofer won't now do them as he insists we need new soffits and gutters for £4000 plus VAT, though we can get a discount for putting his firm's sign on the scaffolding. He never said this when he

looked at the job last week. We look aghast and explain we don't have spare thousands, even if the soffits do look rather rotten. Nicola takes against him instantly. "He's just the sort of man who would be employing modern slaves," she says.

I manage to write a match review for my West Ham blog, but it's a day of distractions. The extension is finished next door, but now their Polish builders want access to the drain in our extension as there's a damp patch on the new wall. This would involve taking down some plasterboard, so they agree to consult an expert. Then I have to use my printer to scan some documents for Nicola who is applying for an Irish passport because her grandfather was born there and she doesn't want to be part of Brexit Britain.

Then we help our neighbour Si, who is locked out of her house and asks to sit in our living room. We try phoning and emailing her son and daughter and eventually the problem is solved. I put the electric heater on in my office area, though I have to turn it off whenever Nicola walks through, as she doesn't allow heating until November. She does allow me to put the central heating on timer for our lodgers though, as I point out they might expect warmth for £30 a night. Lola then arrives for our Monday family dinner and we chat over a pint of Proper Job and a glass of Sauvignon.

Tuesday October 29
Better progress on starting my music biographies and writing up some of my planned Lake District book — it's best to get my memories down quickly before they fade. There are now four sample chapters so that's enough to try with a publisher and I'm developing a format with a synopsis of fells bagged, buses used and places stayed at the start of each chapter.

Book Group is in the Ecology Centre in the evening, where we discuss the book version of *Gentleman Jack* and lesbian frolics with Miss Walker over shared drinks, hummus and cheese.

Wednesday October 30

A surprise tweet from a reader called Nikki who has sent me a picture of a Hippo, referencing my book *There's A Hippo in My Cistern,* which was published way back in 2008. It's touching that it's still being thought of 11 years later. We have a tweet exchange and Nikki says, "I found it to be one of those books you can't put down. There's many laugh out loud moments that's for sure, I particularly enjoyed the chicken guarding." Shakespeare had his Sonnets, but I have my chicken-guarding fox-chasing epic to be remembered by.

Thursday October 31

Sold five paperbacks and eight e-books on KDP this month, earning £27.70 in royalties, plus $2.93 for an American sale. Write three potted biographies of jazz artists. These are the hardest to do as jazz musicians have long careers and form endless quintets and trios while recording a live album seemingly every week — while as a fan of concise pop songs I find jazz meanders on forever.

Then I get the organic vegetables from the reservoir, take them home and go out again to meet Nicola at the Lexington in Stoke Newington. She's been writing a climate change column for the *Islington Gazette,* which is free, though she does get paid for photos. Now the editor is leaving for the *Huffington Post* and she's not sure if her column will be retained.

We meet local green councillor Caroline Russell at the bar, who has just had her electric bike nicked, plus

Richard Watts the leader of Islington Council. We chat to some of the journalists and hope that the new editor will know the area rather than being dropped in. At least we still have two decent newspapers in our borough; so many of them have closed around the country adding to the army of unemployed journalists. And so ends the month, not with a whimper but a pint of Camden Pale.

NOVEMBER

**IN POD WE TRUST — IRISH WIFE — BORIS
DANCING — NEVER MIND THE BUS STOPS —
HOW TO BE A MAN — WAITING FOR THE
GREAT LEAP FORWARDS — WEST HAM
LEGENDS — A VERY BRITISH COOP**

Monday November 4

Nicola leaves to take the train to Budapest for a
conference on positive journalism. In a right
result, she's getting her train fare paid. I'm left at
home to walk Vulcan and defend the house against foxes.
Lodger Tom is away this week, though lodger Luciana
will be here and out of the house by seven each morning
to do her proper job as a civil servant. West Ham suffered
a terrible home defeat to Newcastle on Saturday and I
write it up for my Hammers blog, though it might not
count as positive journalism, even if it is cathartic. Do my
first music biography of the week on Clairo, an American
indie singer.

In the evening go to the pub quiz with the lads at the
Faltering Fullback. An inspired Woody remembers that
Jane Seymour played Solitaire in *Live and Let Die* and
that bananas are the second most popular fruit sold
worldwide after tomatoes. Adrian's musical mind palace
dredges up Belle and Sebastian as the makers of the
albums *The Boy With the Arab Strap* and *Girls in
Peacetime Want to Dance*. We also deduce that *Radio-
activity*, *Robot* and *Tour de France* were Kraftwerk
albums and I'm rather pleased to identify Hearts as the
team that sacked manager Craig Levein. With just four

players our Beta Males side finishes second and wins £30.

Tuesday November 5

Walk the dog. Write up my Beta Males review. Then my keyboard dies — the shift key is not working and I waste half a day swapping keyboards and Googling keyboard problems. I end up ordering a new one from the Apple store at Covent Garden for £99. Take delivery of a couple of boxes of *The Pavement* for Nicola and an Amazon book for her.

At 4pm comedian Phil Whelans phones to ask me to do a West Ham podcast for Stop! Hammer Time. He apologises for the short notice but they've been let down. I take the train to Kings Cross and meet Phil and Jim, first in the pub and then in an office, where we sit around microphones as I chat to Phil and fellow compere Jim. It's unpaid but fun, and I doubt if the presenters get anything either. Like everything else, there's the hope that one day it might turn into something lucrative.

As ever it's enjoyable to natter about West Ham and the ageing Pablo Zabaleta seeming to have been caught in a time loop as he's outpaced by Newcastle's Saint-Maximin. The podcast must have been good, as travelling home I see fireworks going off all over London.

Wednesday November 6

Walk Vulcan and stop for a coffee. Then waste half a day having to pick up my new keyboard from the Apple Store at Covent Garden. Oh for the office days of having an IT department. Back home to write a music biography and do a West Ham blog post.

In the evening go to see my daughter Lola talk at Outlandish Space4, a 'hub' for the creative arts in Finsbury Park. She is very impressive and talks with humour and lucidity about editing her magazine *The Fight Continues* and her spoken word events and outlets for the mag. But as for being an editor — don't do it! Several other inspiring young people talk, a 16-year-old who organised a campaign against education budget cuts, plus people from the Student Climate Network and the social enterprise Creative Opportunities. I'm by some distance the oldest person there, but enjoy my role as Lola's venerable dad.

Thursday November 7

Made 36p on AdSense! Do three more music biographies on Dutch singer Emma Heesters, American Christian rockers Sidewalk Prophets and K-Pop star Baek-a-yeon. I never knew there was so much music in the world. I've interviewed another Pilates teacher for the newsletter and tweak my copy with some changes the teacher has suggested then write up a news item for my round-up of Pilates stories. Get the organic veggies before Nicola returns from Budapest, full of positive journalism anecdotes.

Friday November 8

Retrieve a chewed-up white stiletto that the fox has left in our garden along with a chewed yogurt pot. There's a mangled trainer in the front garden as well. Does the fox have a foot fetish? Let the chickens out of their inner coop and scatter them some seed. Nicola says the crack in the living room is getting bigger plus there's a new one in Nell's old bedroom. Hang the washing up and do a West Ham blog post. Walk the dog and bump into our friend Rachel while Vulcan and myself are in the Park Theatre café. She is busy editing her book on starting an orchestra. Rachel, who now lives mainly in France, also edited my book *Football and its Followers*, so we enjoy a brief chat as I ask her if she is still ruthlessly cutting bad puns, as she did for my works.

Email John the editor of *Lakeland Walker* who is also having problems freelancing, as he's been chatting to the washing machine repair-man for an hour about music. He wants to see my proposal about a feature on the best mountains to walk by bus.

Write a West Ham summary for the *Observer* in return for a blog and book plug but no cash. Look for a map of York, get the suitcase out of the attic and pack for our visit to Nell tomorrow.

Saturday November 9 — Monday November 11
Enjoy a long weekend staying in an Air B&B cottage in York and visiting Nell at her university. We haven't seen her for eight weeks. Lola joins us too and we reunite for a family dinner. Nell is enjoying nightclubbing so much that she's late to meet us at the station, which is a good sign, if I remember my own dissolute student days correctly. The tight medieval streets of York look lovely on a cold York afternoon as we explore the Shambles and walk round the Minster. We explore the Jorvik Viking museum and the Merchant Adventurers' Hall, eat in numerous cafés and enjoy pints in the Golden Fleece.

Tuesday Nov 12
Write up some Pilates research for the latest Pilates newsletter and send the copy off to owner Bill and designer Jim for approval. Send my West Ham answers off to the *Observer*. Go to the W B Yeats pub in the evening with Nicola and Paula as Nicola's Irish passport has come through. She celebrates with half a pint of Guinness (not sure she quite gets being Irish yet) and tells me that as her husband I will be allowed to emigrate to Ireland and, as a writer, be exempt from tax. Not that I

pay it here either, as my income is so low. We drink a toast to W B Yeats and hope that things don't fall apart after Brexit.

Wednesday Nov 13
Vivian from the Newham Bookshop phones asking me if I can interview the *Guardian's* John Crace about his new book at her event next Friday. Sadly I can't do it, as it clashes with my visit to hear the 'West Ham Legends' speak at the Brentwood Centre. My tickets were a birthday present from Nicola back in August and I don't want to let her down by not going.

Thursday November 14
More remnants of scattered foil left in the garden by the fox. Complete my music biographies on four Americans in Travis McCoy, Boys Like Girls, Gary Bartz and Gene Russell plus French rocker Jean-Louis Aubert. Get the organic veggies from the reservoir and cook dinner for when Nicola returns from teaching riding.

Friday November 15
Prime Minister Boris Johnson is in trouble for not visiting flood victims in South Yorkshire. So I send an idea to the *Guardian's* Short Cuts column, linking this to last month's Islington Sylvanian Families flood and wondering if his tardy response might lose him the election. The Islington tsunami damaged 250 homes. Water poured into the basement of the Sylvanian Families shop and manager Ben Miller-Poole had to scramble around trying to save the stock of miniature animal figures. Miller-Poole saved as many Sylvanians as he could but the next day parents and children looked on in horror as damaged figures were placed on the pavement waiting to be destroyed. Despite being a former local, at

least until his own family life became less than Sylvanian, there was no visit from Boris and no offer of counselling to the bereaved Hedgehog, Chocolate Rabbit and Walnut Squirrel Families.

I suggest that maybe Dominic Cummings can help Boris by organising a belated trip to the Sylvanian Families shop, an honour for the heroic Mr Miller-Poole, a photo op with the Marshmallow Mouse Family and a pledge of more Sylvanian flood defences. I think it's a half-decent idea, but there's no response.

Nicola phones in a panic before holding her seminar at Elephant and Castle. She has forgotten some vital notes, which I have to photo and then WhatsApp to her. Make some progress writing my *Diary of a Nobody* sample chapters.

Monday November 18
Never mind the bus stops... Write up my mountains by bus idea and send it to *Lakeland Walker,* for possible use in the spring issue. There's much to be said for fell-walking by bus in true Alfred Wainwright style, while it's also stopping Lakeland gridlock and avoiding car parking scrambles. My proposal gets pretty enthusiastic about climbing Barf from the X5, Castle Crag via the 78 and High Rigg from the 555.

Tuesday November 19
Send off some invoices and write two music biogs. Finish reading *How To Be a Woman* by Caitlin Moran. It's enjoyable, though I can't help but raise a wry smile when she says that during a crisis of confidence her agent had to visit her eight times at her house. Eight times! No agent has ever been to my house — and if they did it would probably be to ask where my manuscript is, because it was due in last week. Midlist writers are

certainly not high-maintenance and the only writer's block I've known was the tower block I lived in at Westbourne Park in the 1980s.

Thursday November 21

Take Lola to see Billy Bragg play at the Islington Assembly Rooms. Outside there's my old mate Chip selling booklets of picket line poetry. We know each other from Red Wedge days back in the 1980s and Chip is now the poetry editor of the *Morning Star* — another unpaid gig. No-one goes into socialism for the money. Inside there's Scouser-turned-Essex-resident Kevin, another old friend from the 1980s, whom I interviewed in my book *The Joy of Essex*. At the bar we find ourselves discussing West Ham's slump with a couple of other blokes from Essex. "This gig is entirely full of dads from Essex who support West Ham," remarks Lola in a tone of wonderment.

I've been watching Billy Bragg play for nearly 40 years. My late friend Paul and myself started our fanzine *Notes From Underground* after seeing him play above a pub near Piccadilly Circus and Billy was my first interview for the 'zine. I interviewed him for *LAM* magazine too, in my first job. As ever he's full of upcoming election banter and Essex humour. Billy says we have to lose our cynicism. Lola loves *New England* and I reminisce to *Must I Paint You a Picture* and *Waiting For The Great Leap Forwards*. That song starts with a sense of defeat, but slowly moves into something much more inspirational. It's not the time to give up.

Friday November 22

Coffee at Lola's café, where we discuss last night's concert. She was the youngest person by 20-odd years. Back home I go through my sample Lake District chapters and the chapters I have for my *Diary of a Writing Nobody* idea, trying to work out if they are any good and how I sell them to a publisher. Go through old Family articles in back copies of the *Guardian,* looking for ideas. When it was a pull-out section there was a lot more opportunity for my style of gentle reflections on family life. Now the Family section is just two pages in the magazine and it's moved on to more sensational stories about children dying, discovering your dad was a Nazi or your mum was your sister, the sort of thing which no doubt attracts readers but is difficult to write about without personal experience.

Forget about writing for a bit and head off to Essex with my pal Fraser, the Raymond Chandler of Ilford crime writing, to watch four 'West Ham Legends' speak at the Brentwood Centre. Fraser is another journalist turned author, trying to find an agent for his crime novel having completed an MA in Creative Writing.

The venue is some distance out of Brentwood in a sports hall, but Trevor Brooking, Tony Gale, Frank McAvennie and Julian Dicks put on a fine, indiscreet performance with lots of anecdotes on broken curfews and dressing room japes. Then it's a taxi back to Brentwood and a long train journey back into London.

Saturday November 23
None of the current West Ham team play like legends as they lose 3-2 at home to Spurs, with goalkeeper Roberto again playing woefully.

Monday November 25
Write up my West Ham Legends visit and the Spurs match review for my blog. Then it's Graham Parker at the Union Chapel with my pal Robert, plus Denis from the *Guardian* and another old friend from Red Wedge days,

Hilary and her partner Michael. It's not Graham's best set and he doesn't do *You Can't Be Too Strong*, but the acoustics are great in this atmospheric venue and it's good to see some old friends.

Tuesday November 26
Ben Bradman has been in touch and asked me to spend a day on ideas to promote the book by the wellness app MD. I come up with various stunt ideas for surveys, transforming well-known landmarks and roping in suitable celebrities. Getting paid for ideas is always satisfying.

Wednesday November 27
A further part of the ceiling surround has fallen down in the living room, landing on the dvd player. I sweep up the plaster dust with a brush and remove the chunks of ceiling surround to the cellar. The chicken shed door is still sticking and the roof is sagging, while the guttering is leaking at the back of our house. Nicola has recruited a handyman called Johnny who does a bit of drilling holes in pieces of wood from the cellar and then miraculously fixes the chicken shed, doing in half an hour what it would have taken me a decade to do.

Thursday November 28
Music biographies completed. This week it's been Argentine ska band Los Autenticos Decadentes, British jazz singer Annie Ross, Puerto Rican sex symbol Barbie Rican, Danish rapper Benny Jamz and Norwegian rocker Jonas Fjeld. Now that's what I call eclectic.

Friday November 29
Sales of *Man About Tarn* seem to be going up. This month it's sold 13 paperbacks and ten e-books, netting

£52 in royalties, plus $1.10 in the US and six cents in Canada for pages read on Kindle Unlimited. It must be the Christmas market giving it a boost and it's encouraging that for the second Christmas running it's still being sent as a gift.

Saturday November 30
Go to Chelsea versus West Ham with Fraser. One of my football book group pals has blagged us a couple of tickets in the Chelsea stand. We keep quiet, but incredibly West Ham, winless for eight games, beat the Blues 1-0 and rookie keeper David Martin keeps a clean sheet on his debut, breaking down in tears at the end and running to his dad Alvin, a former Hammers star. That's what playing for West Ham should mean. There's surely hope for us all.

DECEMBER

GRAVEYARD SHIFT — LAST TANGO IN HALIFAX — BORIS GETS THE ELECTION DONE — CHRISTMAS CAPERS — SANTA BRINGS THE SACK — SECRET AGENT DOWN THE PUB — AMAZON AGGRO

Sunday December 1

Nicola takes me on a trash archaeology walk around Finsbury Park. It's for an art project to highlight waste in our society. We don gloves and pick up cans of beer, fireworks, train tickets, ice cream sticks, bottle tops and numerous other bits of muddy rubbish before depositing them in finds bags. Then we move on to the Parkland Walk to meet Denis, Clare and son Fin for a walk towards Crouch End. Denis is trying to de-stress through nature after too much work; I've spent much of the year trying to de-stress through too little.

Monday December 2

Ben Bradman seems to have found me a dead-end job. He wants me to think up PR ideas to promote a new bespoke funeral service. No doubt he wants me to work the graveyard shift. Could well be a nice little urn-er.

The Beta Males win the first prize of £50 at the Faltering Fullback. We quickly crack the picture round theme of celebrities who have supported political parties and I'm pleased to identify Ian Callaghan as the player who has made most appearances for Liverpool; and to know that the Clash drummer Terry Chimes was known as Tory Crimes and then utilise the green theme to ascertain that Billie Joe Armstrong was in Green Day. It's single malt all round after the scores come through.

Wednesday December 4
Complete my funeral ideas for Ben, including bizarre coffins, modern grave goods, designer urns, euphemisms for death, songs about death, death cafes and a lot of other deadly-interesting stuff. It's been fun working on death.

Thursday December 5
Do a phone interview with Shelly, a Pilates teacher, for the newsletter. Complete my music biographies. This week it's been Canadian country singer Andrew Hyatt, Chinese singer Jason Zheng, Italian pop singer Cesare Cremoni, UK house act Goodboys and early American rappers the Sugarhill Gang. Send out a Facebook post/begging letter for the Christmas market: "Buy or sell books... If anyone wants a signed copy of *Man About Tarn* to give as an Xmas present then I have copies in my lock-up. Ditto *Goodbye to Boleyn*, *The Joy of Essex*, *Whovian Dad* and *There's a Hippo in My Cistern*. Just message to arrange." It works fairly quickly, as my pal Lindsay in Brussels orders a copy of *The Joy of Essex* for her Essex Girl colleague at the EU.

Friday December 6
Another call from Ben Bradman who wants me to do two hours on ideas connected with a sweary celebrity chef. Someone has to effing do it, even if it is a kitchen nightmare.

Saturday December 7 — Monday December 9
Take the train to Halifax for our wedding anniversary.

Have to break the news to Nicola that it's Halifax, Yorkshire, not Halifax, Nova Scotia. Actually it's very on trend since Sally Wainwright's *Gentleman Jack* has been on TV and it's now encountering a boom in lesbian tourism, among other visitors. Plus there have been four series of *Last Tango in Halifax,* also by Sally Wainwright, chronicling the septuagenarian romance between Alan and Celia and their somewhat dysfunctional families. 'Appen it's rather a happening place.

We meet up with Nell who is joining us for the afternoon and visit Shibden Hall where Anne Lister lived and planned her saucy romps with Miss Walker. Plus there's the fantastic former wool market of Piece Hall, now full of galleries of shops selling Yorkshire soap and stocking fillers and a massive former mill converted into an art gallery in Dean Clough. We find some good beer, everyone's friendly and it's all much more real and better value than a lot of the mini-breaks down south with their Christmas markets. I guess we'll always have Halifax.

Tuesday December 10
West Ham lost 3-1 at home to Arsenal last night and I write up the match for my West Ham blog. Start writing up the final copy for the December Pilates newsletter. I've got the teacher interview, plus bits about Pilates being tried by the *Guardian's* Zoe Williams, Leslie Ash using it to aid her recovery from MSSA, facial Pilates, a smoothie recipe and some festive gift ideas. Nell arrives home from York for the Christmas holidays.

Wednesday December 11
Work on the music biographies today. This week it's J-Pop stars World Order, rapper Melle Mel, cult football fan the Wealdstone Raider, American pop singer Agatha

Lee Monn and German schlager singer Costa Cordalis, known for such epic tracks as *Carolina, Komm*.

Thursday December 12

It's General Election day. Walk to the church to cast my vote early doors. Nell says she doesn't know anyone in the world who votes Tory. It doesn't mean they won't win though. Labour's campaign has been much worse than in 2017 when they nearly won. There seems to have been a new policy announcement every day and the anti-Semitism allegations haven't helped. Jeremy Corbyn looks tired too and has sat on the fence over Brexit. In contrast Boris just wants to get Brexit done. Surely the nation can't vote for Brexit? It won't be done for a year and then it's likely to be a no-deal. Will there be some miraculous swing back towards Jezza?

At ten pm its deep depression as the exit poll predicts a massive Tory majority and massive Conservative inroads into Labour's 'red wall'. Nicola still has to go and help the Green Party at the count at the Sobell Centre as the Tories pop champagne.

Friday December 13

Boris is triumphant. To make it worse the subsidence men arrive to take more readings and both my house and my dreams of solid foundations on the parliamentary road to socialism start to crumble. Read the papers and look at the BBC News for the analysis. A cabinet of yes men and women is set to be appointed. Take a walk with Nicola and Vulcan along the Parkland Walk to Highgate to try and clear our heads. Five years of Boris Johnson being king of the world. The only compensation is that he has to give something beyond austerity to the former Labour voters who voted for him.

Saturday December 14
Do a guided tour of the Caledonian Market clock tower with Nicola. We have to climb a number of interior ladders through several floors. I resist the urge to jump off, though I do suffer vertigo near the top on a suspended stair and decline to walk on the balcony outside. Then on to the pub with Matt and Lisa to watch West Ham, astonishingly, win 1-0 at Southampton

Sunday December 15
A Christmas carol service at St Mellitus church in Finsbury Park, featuring an orchestra playing Bach and other classics. Half way through Jeremy Corbyn takes his pew. He receives a standing ovation and a chorus of, "For he's a jolly good fellow". Stanley, our octogenarian friend and *Evening Standard* deliverer, goes to shake Jeremy's hand. His wife wipes away a tear. Corbyn might be slightly worse than Pol Pot according to the *Daily Mail*, but he's still popular in Islington.

Monday December 16
Our first week in Boris's Britain begins. Send invoices for my Pilates newsletter and the last set of music biographies before Christmas. Send a pitch for a feature on the 30th anniversary of Philosophy Football, purveyors of quirky tee-shirts, to the *Guardian, Four-Four-Two* and the *New Statesman*. Go to Lidl to buy some ingredients for our family Christmas dinner with Nell, Lola and her new boyfriend Michael, plus friends Kimi and Paula in our kitchen.

Tuesday December 17
Pitch an idea of a feature on Halifax to the Travel section of the *Guardian.* Then write up a series of answers on West Ham for the *Observer's* half-season fans' round-up.

As usual there's no reward beyond the oxygen of publicity. I'm fairly scathing about West Ham's slump into a relegation struggle and the lack of a decent reserve goalkeeper.

Wednesday December 18
My last music biographies before Christmas are sent off to e-space. They're on country acts the Good Lovelies and Johnny Reid, plus the more complicated profiles of jazz artists Mike Holober, Bill Connors and Brian Lynch. Go to see the rather contrived seasonal movie *Last Christmas* with Nicola.

Friday December 20
Time to send some Christmas cards... Annoyingly *Guardian Sport* has published a piece on Philosophy Football. I should have probably sent my idea direct to Sport rather than the Short Cuts and magazine sections I tried. And I could have submitted it earlier. Have I taken my eye off the ball with the Pilates and music biography work? Am I stretched too thinly? Should I jack in the music biographies? Time to reassess after Christmas.

Saturday December 21
A Christmas party at Hilary and Michael's house in Crouch End. Journalism has helped make me make some good friends. I know Hil from Red Wedge days and then her time at *Time Out*. Denis, another old *Time Out* journo and now at the *Guardian,* is there too. Plus Chip, another old Red Wedger and Phil, who covers Wycombe for BBC Sport and knows one of my old LCC students. Thankfully no-one asks me what book I'm working on, though the round of Christmas parties has begun.

Sunday December 22

My West Ham summary appears on the *Observer,* which at least makes me look impressive. We all go to Stratford to see Auntie Kaz having for some reason booked tickets to see the movie *Cats.* Imagine Ray Winstone with pointed ears in a feline jump suit and be assured it gets much worse. By the end I never want to see another singing cat again.

Monday December 23
Presents sorted, work finished, I do some work on my book idea. Do I just go ahead and write the bloody thing? Send my last Xmas cards. Buy beer, wine and potatoes. *Man About Tarn* has sold £80 worth of books in December so far. It's encouraging that it doesn't seem to have a limited shelf-life.

Tuesday December 24
Over to Lola's house in Turnpike Lane, where Granny Fiona and Anthony have arrived to stay for our family Christmas. Then back to Highbury for our book club friend Sue's Christmas drinks. Meet a man who used to do the fire-regulation testing for West Ham. A few people ask me what book I'm working on and I say I'll have to kill them if I tell them, before retreating to the beer bucket.

Wednesday December 25
As Noddy Holder once hollered, it's Christmas!!! First it's church, which Nicola likes, and wishing 'peace be with you' to our neighbours in the pews. Then it's opening presents and champagne in the living room. This year lunch is at our house, with Nicola and our daughters plus Nicola's mum Fiona and partner Anthony. They bring over a turkey for the meat-eaters while my nut roast is successful thanks to a new moist formula. Then we

settle down to watch the *Gavin and Stacey* Christmas special.

Thursday December 26

How very considerate. Amazon Associates emailed yesterday, on Christmas Day, to tell me: "Your Associates account is at risk of closure. We reviewed your account as part of our ongoing monitoring of the Amazon Associates Program. To complete our review, we need you to provide more information about how you're referring customers to the Amazon Site."

They then ask for "a detailed description of the methods you are using to refer traffic to the Amazon Site by providing: A list of all Sites on which your Special Links or banner ads are posted, including social media accounts; Advertising services you are using; Links to screenshots of your Site's analytics tools that show your Site traffic and its sources; The keywords you are using to drive referrals; Any plugins or browser add-ons you use; A sequence of links that allows us to duplicate the clicks the majority of your customers make to get to the Amazon Site via your Special Links; Any other information that would be relevant to confirming your compliance with the Operating Agreement."

Through Amazon Associates I receive a few pence every time someone orders a book via my blog. My Amazon Associates balance currently stands at £2.83. A very merry Christmas to you too, Jeff Bezos.

Friday December 27

Spend most of the day setting up a Black and Decker Workmate that Nicola has given me for Christmas. In her defence I did ask for it to help saw up the tonnes of wood the Wood Man has left us. Have to watch a YouTube video first, as there are a fiendish number of parts. DIY does not come easily. As a workman I'd be earning even less than a writer. But when the Workmate is finally assembled it has two clamping sections that can hold tight a piece of wood to saw. I set to work trying to saw some of the thousands of pieces of wood the Wood Man has left on our doorstep during the year. We watch *Paddington 2* in the evening, in which Hugh Grant is excellent. We love his line, "Stage combat, level 4!"

Saturday December 28
Email my reply to Amazon Associates detailing my blogs, attaching a screengrab of my blog analytics and telling them I am not sure what a keyword is, I have no idea what a plug-in or browser ad-on is and I have very little idea about the technical questions they are asking. I also suggest that, "unless Amazon Associates is being run by Ebenezer Scrooge, I'd suggest not sending emails threatening to close my account on Christmas Day. It's meant to be the season of goodwill."

Watch West Ham lose 3-1 at home to Leicester. Manager Manuel Pellegrini is sacked an hour later and loud cheers ring out in the bar where we're drinking afterwards. After a couple of pints and some mournful contemplation of relegation retreat home to do the match review on my blog and review the likely candidates to replace Pellegrini. By AdSense standards it's almost lucrative, as with interest piqued, my post makes 72p.

Sunday December 29
Nicola and myself head out for birthday drinks with Ursula, one of the trustees of Islington Faces. We're at the Alwyne near Highbury Corner and the bar is full of fans from the Arsenal versus Chelsea game. There's a table of soccerati types having some snacks and beers. "Nicola, I think that's David Luxton over there... shall I

say hello?"

He's the agent who got me a good deal for *There's a Hippo In My Cistern* back in 2008 and also negotiated a contract for Nicola with her book *Home Made Kids*, though he's not gone for any of our ideas since. The relationship between agents and commissioning editors and writers is always a little awkward, as they hold your career in their hands. It's hard not to feel a little like Alan Partridge pitching to Tony Hayers.

When I approach David, he's friendly and pleased to see both Nicola and myself. I manage to get *Man About Tarn* and my West Ham book *Goodbye to Boleyn* into the conversation and at no point does he suspect that I might harbour plans to kidnap him and keep him imprisoned in my cellar until he agrees to push one of my ideas.

Still, from David's viewpoint, I can see that as he only gets ten or 15 per cent of any deal, anything he takes on has to get a decent advance. *There's a Hippo in my Cistern* sold 2700 or so copies, which was ok, but is never going to make him or me rich. And with advances getting lower and lower, 15 per cent of nothing isn't going to be any use to him. But perhaps this is a sign. Barring some kind of global pandemic, maybe I'll work with him again, or find another agent. And with West Ham struggling again perhaps he'd like a book on the Hammers' greatest relegations?

Monday December 30

Finish reading *The Bromley Boys*, a very funny book by Dave Roberts that was a Christmas present from Nell. It's about supporting a rubbish non-league team, when Roberts' was an impressionable 15-year-old in the 1960s. Every book gives some kind of inspiration, and this gentle comedy of feel-bad nostalgia gives me a few ideas. *Man About Tarn* has done well this month, my KDP report reveals a stonking 38 paperbacks and seven e-books sold to Christmas buyers, netting £98 in royalties plus $3.45 from an Australian sale.

Tuesday December 31
Paula and her daughter Izzy come over, along with Lola and we all watch Jools Holland on TV trying to keep up with Stormzy and co and celebrating the arrival of a New Year. Another year over and a new one begun; 2019 began with a crisis of confidence, but a lot has been achieved: a new bionic eye; a new tooth; features in *The Author* and *Lakeland Walker*; Nell getting three As and starting university; Nicola's exhibition; Lola's magazine; I made it to 60; this jobbing writer found two new jobs and did some ghost-writing on wellness; my income has gone up a little; I've been to see a life-coach; four trips to the Lake District and an idea for a book; our Sarlat sojourn; trips to Halifax and York; and I've now written a lengthy proposal for a book version of my *Diary of a Writing Nobody* feature, which I might call *What Are Words Worth?*

JANUARY — FEBRUARY 2020

DEATH OF A SALESMAN — TERMINATED — LONDON CALLING — REINSTATED — CLIMB EVERY WAINWRIGHT — NOT FOR US — GOING VIRAL — PAYING TO PUBLISH

Wednesday January 1

All is quiet on New Year's Day. The radio says that a new mutant virus has crossed over from animals to humans via a market in Wuhan in China. But that's a long way away and no doubt it will be contained like Sars. Nicola wants us to try Vegan-ary and cut out milk, butter and cheese. Take a walk along the Lea Valley with Nicola and Paula, heading from Clapton to Tottenham Hale. The River Lea is surprisingly unspoilt here, with its grassy banks, meanders and woodland. To get the New Year off to a good start we have a fine mushroom burger in the riverside Cafe at Stamford Hill. Then it's on to West Ham versus Bournemouth for David Moyes' first game in charge. Astonishingly West Ham win 4-0. Never in doubt!

Thursday January 2
Write up the Bournemouth match for my West Ham blog. Nicola and myself take the tube to the matinee of *Death of a Salesman* at the Piccadilly Theatre. It's a brilliant play exposing the underbelly of the American Dream, and I've loved it since first studying it at university. Really

Willy Loman is just a freelancer trying to close a deal in the gig economy...

Friday January 3
Send out my West Ham answers to the Manchester University PhD student who has requested my help with his thesis on the stadium move. Every writer likes a bit of academic kudos. Then I query the form that has arrived from the bibliographic services company for whom I write the music biographies. It's all been based on trust so far, but now they want me to assign all intellectual property rights to them, and probably my dog and chickens too. They also require me to warrant that "nothing obscene, blasphemous, libellous or otherwise objectionable or illegal" will be included which is worrying, as they are compiled from online sources and can't all be fact-checked.

After a chat with the Society of Authors there's an email exchange with one of the directors. I'm reassured that it's only a safeguard to ensure that I won't republish the biographies elsewhere and won't deliberately sabotage them with libellous statements. They can't have ever listened to the Sex Pistols or any drill rappers, whose very *raison d'etre* was surely to be obscene, blasphemous, libellous, objectionable and illegal. In the end I agree to sign for a quiet life on the assumption that I will stop doing them soon when better-paid work arrives.

Monday January 6
The house is a little lonely now Nell has returned to York University after the Christmas holiday. Back to work again. Re-send my Halifax and Philosophy Football ideas to several publications. Write an introduction on the challenge of climbing all the Wainwright fells for my possible follow-up to *Man About Tarn*. With an

introduction, a synopsis and four chapters ready it should be ready to send to a few publishers.

Tuesday January 7
More interesting music biographies to do this week, four of the seven are a sub-set of *Monty Python*-related people. The Pythons themselves and their LPs of the TV shows, plus Neill Innes, his brilliant spoof band The Rutles and Innes' previous band the Bonzo Dog Doo Dah Band, who had a hit during my childhood with *I'm The Urban Spaceman*. Find myself somewhat distracted playing Innes' excellent parody of John Lennon, *How Sweet To be an Idiot*.

Wednesday January 8
A cheery note from Amazon Associates:

Effective today, Amazon is terminating your Associates account as well as the Operating Agreement that governs it. Why? We previously issued you a non-compliance warning regarding your Associates account. You did not respond or come into compliance within the specified time. You must stop using the Content and Amazon Marks and promptly remove all links to the Amazon site.

Because you are not in compliance with the Operating Agreement, Amazon will not pay you any outstanding advertising fees. Please be aware that any other related accounts may be closed without payment of any fees. If you've come into compliance this closure may be appealable.

Warmest Regards, Amazon Associates

Love the "Warmest Regards" at the end. It's all rather baffling, as I have used Amazon Associates for many years without any previous problems. My account actually made the £25 threshold and I received a grand sum of £28 last year. I immediately lodge an appeal likening the situation to Josef K in *The Trial,* where I am accused of some form of non-compliance, but no-one is telling me what it is. I also point out that I have been commissioned to write two books for Amazon by their Kindle Single section, *Whovian Dad* and *Man About Tarn.*

I trawl through the small print of the compliance conditions and discover that the problem might be they want me to insert the words, "As an Amazon Associate I earn from qualifying purchases" into the widgets advertising my books. If only they had said... so I dutifully insert the required statements on to my blogs hoping this might get me reinstated into a scheme that has made me £2.83 in nine months.

Thursday January 9
It's my football book club meeting at the Pizza Express at the South Bank, with Peter and the two Tonys. We discuss David Goldblatt's massive work *The Age of Football,* though none of us has got beyond half-way. It certainly gets over the astonishing level of corruption in world football, though my own ethics lapse too as Vegan-ary is shelved for a cheesy pizza. Nicola and myself have already cheated a little by finishing off that Lidl Stilton in the fridge.

Friday January 10
One small victory for freelance man... I have been reinstated by Amazon Associates! The Amazon email says:

Thank you for your cooperation in complying with the terms of the Operating Agreement. As a result of your response, your Associates account has been reinstated. Please note, due to your violations of our Operating Agreement, the withheld Advertising fees are not eligible for reinstatement. Your continued participation in the Associates Programme indicates your acceptance of and agreement to comply with the terms of the Operating Agreement. Thank you again for your cooperation and for your participation in the Associates Programme. Warmest Regards, Amazon Associates

So basically they have reinstated me to a scheme they never needed to suspend me from, had a human told me what the problem was, and are withholding my advertising fees. Well done, Jeff Bezos, I hope you enjoy that £2.83.

Do a phone interview with one of the Pilates teachers for the newsletter and work on my Lake District book proposal. Then it's over to the Auld Triangle with Nicola, Lisa and neighbour Nick to watch West Ham lose to Sheffield United and be denied a last-minute equaliser by sodding VAR.

Saturday January 11
Go to see the Clash's *London Calling* exhibition at the Museum of London with Nicola. The ice age is coming the sun is zooming in… It's fantastic to see the lyrics of *London Calling* on flyposters outside, set on a brutalist concrete walkway. Inside there's Paul Simenon's smashed guitar from the cover of *London Calling* now displayed in a glass case and I'm very excited to see the band's leather jackets and sleeveless military chic shirts in a display case. Was it really all 40 years ago?

Monday January 13
The Pilates teacher I interviewed has decided she doesn't want the interview to appear. End up doing a big Google

search for new stories.

Wednesday January 15
Cobble together the Pilates newsletter without a teacher interview. I've covered a feature in *Vogue*, a piece in the *Times* on body confidence and wearing make-up for Pilates classes, the *Daily Mail's* snaps of Sharon Hyland and Hailey Bieber at LA Pilates classes, and a book on living longer that recommends Pilates.

Thursday January 16
Complete the week's music biographies. This week it's been seven, six of them are American, country acts Billy Dean, Andy Griggs and Jo Dee Messina, rocker Howie Day, R&B singer Natalie, jazz musician Jack Shelden and most interestingly, Kraut-rockers Brainticket. Influenced by Tangerine Dream, Can and Hawkwind among others, their Sixties and Seventies experimentations include the album *Psychonaut* and a rock opera called *Celestial Ocean*. I'll take whatever they're taking, please.

Friday January 17
A few glitches, but approve the Pilates newsletter after a few exchanges of emails. Write up the marketing proposal for my Lake District book, which I'm tentatively calling *Climb Every Wainwright*. Nicola and I go to see *Shackleton's Stowaway* at our local Park Theatre with Fleur who is visiting the Smoke from Yorkshire again and Andrew from the Beta Males and his partner Jo. It's a play highlighting the relationship between the leader of the Endurance expedition to the Antarctic and his uninvited guest. The wind and snow effects are well-realised as poor old Ernest Shackleton suffers more obstacles and privations than a freelancer trying to get a piece in the *Guardian*.

Monday January 20

A long morning spent on a two-hour phone conference with Nicola, myself and Thomas our sort-of financial adviser. Years ago we took out some ethical investments with a green financial adviser, whose company was taken over by another firm in Manchester. Now they are reviewing our finances and basically deciding that we should part company. Still, Tom is quite patient as we reveal how little we know of the stock market and his endless graphs, and we do make progress on calculating what our state pensions will be and freeing up some cash as our outgoings exceed our incomings — a situation of which Mr Micawber would not approve.

Over to see Lola later at her gaff in Turnpike Lane, where our daughter has organised an evening of negroni cocktails followed by spaghetti and veggie meatballs, ending with crème brulee.

Wednesday January 22

Email my Allendale Dalek idea to the Short Cuts team at the *Guardian* again, about the row between the Museum of Sci-Fi and Allendale Parish Council in Northumberland. The dispute has been going on for two years, in a classic Jobsworths versus Evil Extra-terrestrial Lifeform spat. The latest twist is that the council has admitted it is more worried about the wooden shed housing the Dalek rather than the Dalek itself. So Museum founder Neil Cole is now building a metal Dalek sculpture without a shed, as you do. But clearly the *Guardian's* vision must be impaired, as no reply is forthcoming.

Friday January 24

Do my last music biography of the week on Sleepy

LaBeef, the legendary rockabilly and country singer who has just died at the age of 84. His real name was Thomas LaBeef. He was nicknamed 'Sleepy' because his heavily-lidded eyes made him appear constantly tired. LaBeef was known as 'The Human Jukebox', the title of his 1995 album. At one point he would play 300 shows a year, later cutting this down to a mere 200-250 in the 1990s. There's a lesson in perseverance there.

Saturday January 25
The Foreign Office is advising against all travel to the Hubei Province in China because of the coronavirus outbreak there. Meanwhile West Ham play terribly and lose 1-0 at home to West Brom reserves in the FA Cup. So it's now going to be 40 years without a trophy. It's not the despair, etc.

Monday January 27
Send my *Climb Every Wainwright* book idea to my old agent David. It's probably not commercial enough for him to take on, but having re-established contact just after Christmas it's worth a try. Then book a trip to Grasmere for Nicola and myself in April. I have a plan. If I spend a bit of money and time and take trips to Grasmere, Keswick, Haweswater, Buttermere, Ennerdale and Wasdale this year I can complete all 214 Wainwright fells and have a book ready to publish. Even if I have to self-publish on KDP it will be worthwhile, having established there's a Lakes market.

Friday January 31
Send my *Climb Every Wainwright* idea to Victoria, who is my contact for Amazon's publishing wing, now that my previous editor Andrew has moved on from Kindle Single to Amazon Audible. My KDP report for the month

reveals that I have earned £50.85 in royalties through selling 11 paperbacks and 9 e-books of *Man About Tarn* plus one e-book of *Flying So High* and one of *The Joy of Essex.*

Saturday February 1
The first two cases of coronavirus are confirmed in the UK. Nell WhatsApps to say that a student at York University is one of them. Why does it have to happen at her university? Rumour suggests it's a Chinese student. "Oh no, will I catch it?" asks Nell. The university website is useful and says it's believed the student wasn't on campus, but precautions are being taken. The virus doesn't seem to affect young people too badly, though as Nell has asthma it's still a worry for us.

Monday February 3
Receive a rejection email for *Climb Every Wainwright* from Victoria at Amazon's publishing wing, but it's a nice note: "Thanks so much for this! It's nice to hear from you. Unfortunately I don't think this is for us – we publish in a global way, thinking about the US as much as the UK, and I'm afraid that this idea wouldn't have the resonance there. Best of luck in bringing it to readers though."

My friend Julia (we flatshared back in the 1980s and she's Nell's godmother) has sent me a request from a university lecturer wanting someone to review the book *What You Think You Know About Football* for the journal *Soccer & Society.* I email back with my CV. Only it turns out the lecturer wants me to write for nothing, emailing: "Sorry, no, academic journals don't pay. Sadly, it is often the case that we academics pay to publish. I suppose there is the incentive of a free book?"

I reply politely, that if I had the security of an

academic salary I might do something for free, but as a freelancer I follow NUJ policy and only work for a fee. If academics have to pay to get into journals how long will it be before journalists also have to pay for the privilege of being published?

Friday February 7
A third case of coronavirus has been found in the UK. Go to the dentist for a filling. My dentist says they only have one day's worth of face-masks left as so many people have been panic-buying them in anticipation of a coronavirus epidemic.

Saturday February 8 — Monday February 10
A trip to the Potteries for Stoke City versus Charlton, which I attend with my relatives from my mum's side, Terry and David. The train companies are advising us not to travel this weekend because of Storm Ciara, but after the match I get a lift with David to York, where I meet up with Nicola and Nell in order to celebrate Nell's 19th birthday the next day. She seems pleased we've come up despite the threat of cyclones. We use Dave's house as a base and have a fine weekend, eating brunch in the Cosy Café as rain and wind batters the awnings, taking a walk by the flooding River Ouse and watching the film *1917*. People up here seem a lot less worried about coronavirus than in London, where an atmosphere of panic is setting in.

Wednesday February 12
Send off the final copy for my Pilates newsletter. One day I might even have to start doing it myself, though at £50 a go it's not cheap. This is a good issue, with a piece by a teacher on Pilates being about more than a six-pack, my feature on the famous pictures of Joe Pilates by

photographer Chuck Rapoport, an item on a BBC World Service interview with a teacher who trained with Joseph Pilates, plus a *Telegraph* piece on Meghan Markle and her Pilates guru, and the *Daily Mail's* discovery that Southampton footballer Danny Ings has used Pilates to get back to goalscoring fitness, inspiring my headline, "Ings can only get better".

Friday February 14
Valentine's Day chocolates and coffee for Nicola in bed. Nell has returned home for the weekend and I spend much of the day helping her with her banking options. We go to Nationwide at Crouch End to open a new fixed-term bond. Spend the evening in front of our log-burner as Storm Dennis approaches.

Monday February 17
Nicola and myself take Nell to Kings Cross where she is booked on a cheap 8.30am train. Then we have a good breakfast burger at a café at Coalyard Drop. I move on to visit Waterstone's at Angel to look at the travel section and try to identify likely publishers who might be interested in my *Climb Every Wainwright* book. Some only accept agented works, but I come away with a lengthy list of possibilities.

Monday February 24
Do some re-editing of my updated *Diary of a Nobody* proposal and send it to Biteback. I suspect it's not political enough for them, but they have published me twice before, so it's worth a try.

Lola calls round and is sent to the front garden to admire Nicola's beds of apocalypse-defying chard, potatoes and onions.

"Mum, I think there's a weirdo living in the hedge,

says Lola. "There's a horrible mangled up teddy bear in there."

"Oh, that's for the fox," explains Nicola. "The fox chewed it up there and I've left it out so it can play with it. There's an old trainer out there it likes too." Only in our house...

After dinner we move on to the World's End pub with Lola and her boyfriend Michael, plus my West Ham friends Matt, Lisa and Michael and later-on Nicola. It's slightly weird to be in a pub when everyone is starting to wonder if they are safe. On the big screens we view West Ham take the lead and almost win at unbeatable league leaders Liverpool, only for the Hammers to blow a 2-1 lead after a catastrophic goalkeeping error and then lose 3-2. A familiar melancholy beckons.

Wednesday February 26
Breakfast with house-guest George, a Shrewsbury-based eco-campaigner who still dresses like a character from *An Inspector Calls*. George has been busy tackling climate change denial around the world. Though as he's done a lot of travelling we do wonder if he should hug us goodbye rather than bumping elbows, as someone has suggested.

Thursday February 27
There are now 23 cases of coronavirus in the UK. The fox has left an indeterminate bone on the garden patio. There's still some meat on it and it looks rather like a conceptual work by Damien Hirst. Write up a final biography of the week on the DJ and producer Andrew Wetherall, who has sadly just died. He produced Primal Scream's *Screamadelica*. His influence on acid house rather passed my by in the 1990s, but I'm certainly adding to my musical knowledge through this hack-work.

There's a new report out on nature deficit among children, so I send an idea about my family's history of visiting the Lake District to the Family section of the *Guardian*. Only Steve Chamberlain, my contact on Family, has now gone to work on the *Observer* magazine. He's friendly though, and maybe something will come of this. Then send both my *Diary of a Nobody* and *Climb Every Wainwright* ideas to different sections at the publishers Summersdale. They ignored my *Joy of Essex* proposal a few years ago, but it's still worth a shot as they do a lot of quirky travel and lifestyle books.

Saturday February 29
My KDP report for the month shows £50.85 in royalties through selling nine paperbacks and six e-books of *Man About Tarn* plus one paperback of *Flying So High* and e-books of *Sunday Muddy Sunday and The Joy of Essex*. It's a must-win game at the London Stadium and incredibly West Ham *do* win it, beating Southampton 3-1. During the match I see a fan in the stands wearing a protective mask. A British person has just died on a cruise ship, but surely masks aren't necessary here as yet?

Home to write up the victory on my blog. There's another home game in a fortnight, but there are rumours that large-scale gatherings will soon be closed if the coronavirus takes hold. This is starting to get serious.

MARCH 2020

PANIC ON THE STREETS OF LONDON — LUST HORIZONS — PUB COLLAPSE — LAST TRAIN TO GRASMERE — PISTE OFF — BORIS FELLED — WORKING FOR THE LOCKDOWN — THE DAY THE MUSIC DIED — THE END OF THE WORLD AS WE KNOW IT

Sunday March 1

Hannah from Wales is staying with us and has breakfast with Nicola and myself. We discuss re-wilding over hot porridge, as you do. Watch *Match of the Day* and then go out with Nicola and Vulcan on the Parkland Walk from Finsbury Park to Crouch End, followed by an evening of watching *Doctor Who* and *Last Tango in Halifax*.

Monday March 2

Read a blizzard of financial information from our financial adviser. Start my music biographies. Play for the Beta Males at the Faltering Fullback pub quiz. We're all wondering about social distancing, though after unluckily finishing just outside the money Captain Bob gives us a hug and a handshake, after first wondering if coronavirus is a plot to cull all the oldish folk like us. We remain unsure if there will be a game next month.

Tuesday March 3

The government advises us to wash our hands frequently

with soap and water while singing 'Happy Birthday' twice. Only Boris Johnson seems to be still shaking hands.

Wednesday March 4

Spend two days researching the life of Joseph Pilates for Bill from the Pilates studio. He wants a biography of his major life events to give to actors and playwrights for a possible play on his life. It's some welcome extra cash and an interesting assignment. The German-born Pilates worked in a circus, trained the police and invented his system of exercise while incarcerated as an enemy alien in a camp on the Isle of Man. He then emigrated to America and set up a studio, which was frequented by top ballet dancers and even Christopher Isherwood. Pilates would ask journalists to stand on his chest and challenge them to arm wrestling to prove his fitness. A big character who would make a great subject for a play. I'm in danger of becoming a Pilates expert without ever actually doing it.

Thursday March 5

Complete the five music biographies of the week, including three lengthy and tedious jazz ones, then fetch the organic vegetables and cook dinner for Nicola when she returns from teaching riding.

Friday March 6

Do some work on writing up the summer months of my year in the life of a midlist writer book idea. Write a match review of the Beta Males' pub quiz. Have dinner with Fleur, who is down from Yorkshire and no longer against all terriers. She's here for a Tory women's conference despite coronavirus worries and has some revealing information on how little impact Labour's free broadband pledge had with working class voters in Yorkshire. I wonder whether I should vote for Keir Starmer as the next leader and show her his pledge card. She doesn't want the poster to put in her window though.

Saturday, March 7
It's Arsenal versus West Ham, for once a Hammers game that I can walk to. Meet Lola and her boyfriend Michael in The Gunners Tavern for a pre-match pint, plus Michael's mate and his dad. There's not much social distancing I reflect as I queue at a packed and heaving bar, trying to catch the attention of an overworked barmaid. Is being part of a 60,000 crowd worse than being in a packed pub? Boris Johnson is at the England rugby match so surely things are still ok.

We walk to the ground, up the steps on Drayton Park and around to the huge bustling concourse. Michael's got me a ticket, but it's on my own among the Arsenal fans. I hope the blokes next to me don't have the coronavirus, but who knows? For once West Ham utterly outplay Arsenal and create chance after chance, only for Michail Antonio and Sebastien Haller to miss them all. Predictably Arsenal then get a soft goal that is at first disallowed and only given after a huge wait for VAR. But if West Ham can play like this again they'll surely get out of trouble.

I head back home to wash my hands for 20 seconds before my pal Nigel and his friend Reg with son Henry drop in for a post-match tea, beer and cake with Nicola. We say we'll meet at the Wolves game on Sunday, as long as it's still on.

Fleur arrives back at our house after attending her conference of Conservative women. It went well, she says, even if it's my idea of Room 101. As she's been around politicians all day we don't get too close to her over dinner, lest we catch the virus or even become Tories.

Sunday March 8
Lola and Michael fly off for a mini-break in Barcelona. Italy has closed its borders and the coronavirus situation is worrying in Europe, but they only have to survive four days in Spain. And surely things can't escalate that quickly. Write up yesterday's match for my West Ham blog.

Walk with Nicola to the Cotswold shop at Angel and get some gear for our forthcoming trip to the Lake District, buying a compass, some gloves and a base layer for Nicola. Taking the number 19 bus back, we find the Gunners Tavern is surrounded by police cars and fire engines with the pavement taped off. Part of the roof has collapsed and where I was standing with Lola and Michael yesterday is now a mass of floorboards, bricks and fallen masonry. If it had happened yesterday we might have been killed. It puts coronavirus in perspective, as you don't expect to die having a pint.

Monday March 9
Watch *Match of the Day 2* (West Ham still lose). Start doing the Pilates newsletter and complete my first music biography of the week. Have a coffee at Lola's café and see at close quarters the collapsed roof of the Gunners Tavern, now surrounded by a mass of scaffolding. Watch *The Two Popes* on Netflix with Nicola in the evening.

Tuesday March 10
Work on my Pilates newsletter all day and get the final copy sent away for approval. There has been a theft of all the toilet rolls from the studio's store cupboard, which makes a good final item. Not the bog standard theft. Time

to call in *Broadchurch* CID and deal with wiped records and a tissue of lies. A worldwide pandemic is happening and people steal toilet roll — why?

Wednesday March 11
Do another West Ham blog post on the likelihood of Sunday's game against Wolves being postponed and if it would be the most West Ham relegation ever if we went down because the table was stopped after the next three difficult games with us in the drop zone. Give feedback to a Manchester University MA student who wants some quotes to go with his dissertation on West Ham's ground move. Do the final three music biographies of the week.

Meet Nell at Euston at 21.07 as she arrives home from university carrying two voluminous cases. They tuck you up your mum and dad. Good to see her safely in her bedroom at last.

Thursday March 12
Add an extra paragraph on coronavirus safety in the studio to the Pilates newsletter. A positive rejection email from Biteback Publishing. I knew my *Diary of a Nobody* idea wasn't really their sort of thing, but decided to try anyway having written two books with them. Molly at Biteback writes: "It seems a fantastic idea, one as relatable to writers as it would be readers entangled in the travails of the modern gig economy. We very much enjoyed the extracts you provided and your sense of wry self-deprecating humour really shines through in your prose."

Start packing for the Lakes. Collect the organic vegetables. Cook a family lasagne. Lola comes over and so does Nell's godmother Nicky. Only the coronavirus situation is getting worse. Will Nell's skiing trip take place? She only has to survive a week out there, but the virus is doubling every day. Meanwhile Boris Johnson has announced that, "Many more families will lose loved ones before their time."

Friday March 13
Now Arsenal's manager Mikel Arteta has coronavirus and all Premier League fixtures are cancelled for the next two weeks. The mayoral and local elections have been cancelled for a year, The *Standard* reports that UK coronavirus cases have leapt from 208 to 798 in 24 hours. In Italy the hospitals are overwhelmed.

We spend the morning discussing whether Nell should go skiing, not that we can really stop her. Most businesses in France are now closed. It would save us a lot of worry if the tour company simply called a halt. The Foreign Office is not as yet advising against travelling to France. Nicola manages to get a response from the ski company and they say that the coaches will be at the resort throughout the stay, ready to leave should the resort be closed. This sounds vaguely reassuring. Nell remains determined to go, although are we sending her off to a death sentence? She is at risk through having asthma, even if it is controlled. Her sister Lola is now adamant she shouldn't go and WhatsApping cuttings on the latest death figures from around the world.

But Nell will be at risk in London too, as it's full of people who might have flown in from Wuhan or any other infected area. Someone has already had it at York University. The big worry is if Nell gets marooned in France. Yet she's really looking forward to the trip so should we deny her it? My indecision is final. Nell's isn't and she says she's packing.

Nell has to meet the coach at Chafford Hundred and I go with her to carry her cases. We spray sanitizer on our hands but the commuter train from Stratford is packed and we have to stand and grab handrails in what feels like a festering laboratory of viral disease. At the station I give her a hug goodbye, against advice, and return home on a thankfully near-empty train.

Saturday March 14
The PR industry never stops, not even with a pandemic. Ben Bradman has asked me to spend a couple of hours thinking up ideas for publicising the fact that with lockdown and self-isolation downloads of a sex app he's working for have massively increased. We spend some time earnestly discussing the marketing opportunities to be had from increased masturbation and use of sex toys, before I make my excuses and leave.

Sunday March 15
Supermarkets are saying don't buy more than you need as shelves stand bare... After Nicola has a final paddle boarding session we leave on the 3.24 train to Oxenholme and then on to Windermere and a dog-friendly hotel. Should we even be going? It was booked back in February, but the taxi driver to Grasmere is full of pessimism about the virus and imminent contagion. Still, the room is lovely and faces on to the lake. This could be my last chance to bag some Wainwright fells for a long time.

Monday March 16
Breakfast is good and soon we're off up Steel Fell, another new Wainwright for my wall chart. Meanwhile we've established phone contact with Nell and her ski resort has been ordered to close by the French government. Her coach is returning to the UK tomorrow. At least she's got one day's skiing in.

The visibility is good and we carry on with a circuit

back down to Grasmere via Calf Crag, Gibson Knott and Helm Crag. It's a long steep descent and we're flagging as we descend into the lovely Easedale Road.

At 6pm, just as we reach Grasmere exhausted and desperate for a drink, Lola, who is now our moral arbiter, phones to inform us that Boris Johnson says we should avoid pubs. Reasoning that if we hadn't taken the call and it's not actually banned I race into the Grasmere Inn for a quick pint, which might well be my last in a pub, while Nicola shops at the Co-Op. We're going to eat in our room from now on.

Tuesday March 17
"Are you a bit worried about this virus then?" we overhear one of the staff say at breakfast. It seems a suitably low-key Cumbrian response to the worldwide plague stories emerging on BBC News and the front page of my *Guardian*. The room is empty but another breakfasting couple sit right next to us — the messages aren't getting through yet. Another fine day's walking up past Thirlmere dam and on to the tree-covered summit of Raven Crag. Nell has made it into the coach and is on her way back to London. But this is getting serious. Government adviser Sir Patrick Vallance says that below 20,0000 dead would be a good outcome, while the Chancellor Rishi Sunak is pledging £360 billion to save jobs.

Wednesday March 18
The *BBC News* is still wall-to-wall coronavirus. But it's our last day walking and tomorrow we'll be back in London. Nicola's knees are hurting and she's taking a low-level walk with Vulcan, wandering lonely as a cloud around Grasmere and Rydal Water, taking in Wordsworth's old gaff at Rydal House. Meanwhile I'm

walking up a strangely-deserted path to Grasmere Tarn and then the summit of Seat Sandal. It feels like I'm the last walker in post-apocalyptic Britain, only meeting three other sets of walkers all day. It's a good walk up past a ruined wall to the summit and then down the vast shoulder of Seat Sandal and back to Grasmere.

Just as I'm dreaming of a pint at an outside table at the Good Sport my mobile buzzes. It's Nicola, who says her friend at the boat club says London is about to be shut down completely. She wants to get the train home immediately while there are still trains and no armed checkpoints on the M25. I'm not inclined to believe that the government would do London lockdown without notice, but it seems I am destined never to get a pint.

So it's a rush to book new tickets online, get the bus and then the 8.25pm train from Oxenholme to London. There's a woman with an insistent dry cough in our carriage. Eventually we move compartments. Corona has us all suspecting each other. We stagger out at Euston and take a strangely quiet Victoria line train to Finsbury Park and our house.

Thursday March 19
London has not been locked down. But at least we are back and Nell is here too, to judge by the plates of toast crusts. We have to do some panic-buying as the house is short of food. I avoid Lidl and its long queue of shoppers outside, opting for Sainsbury's to stock up on basics and beer. Invoice Ben Bradman for £50 for the sex app ideas, thinking it might be the last payment I receive for some time. Lola and Michael call round on their bikes, as no-one is using public transport now. We stand two metres away from them as they say they are self-isolating as they have recently returned from Spain.

We also have to stay distanced from Nell as she has

just returned from France on a packed coach full of students. Meanwhile Nicola is stockpiling chickens. She has returned from Freightliners Farm with two hens that actually lay eggs, unlike our elderly Bantams. They are tentatively named Princess Layer and Hennifer Aniston. Only the new chickens seem pretty keen on bullying the smaller Margaret Hatcher and Egg Miliband. Nicola rigs up a barrier between the two warring factions and hopes that this clucking hell will soon pass.

Friday March 20
The schools are closing next week while Lola and Nell's university courses are going online. Nell is going to be stuck with her aged parents until the summer. The pubs and restaurants are closing as Covid-19 gets serious. Both our lodgers are locked down in France so we won't be receiving any more rent, though luckily I can dip into my inherited capital to get us through. Doctors are being asked to come out of retirement. There could be NHS work for Tom Baker at this rate.

Nicola insists on going to the local bike shop before it closes and panic-buys me a new bike, now that we can't use public transport. She also wants us to be able to make a quick getaway in the style of some dystopian road movie. Staying in is the new going out, so we stay in and watch the movie *In Bruges*.

Saturday March 21
Ride my new bike round the park and it's a lot quicker than my old knackered mountain bike. The giant brown chickens are still showing genocidal tendencies towards our bantams Margaret Hatcher and Egg Miliband. Despite the fact they have laid two eggs, Nicola reluctantly returns Princess Layer and Hennifer Aniston to Freightliners Farm as we're too soft to get rid of our

existing useless-at-laying-eggs elderly bantams. We stay in and watch the movie *Arrival*.

Sunday March 22
The girls have home-made Mother's Day cards for Nicola, just like they used to make at primary school. Finish reading *London Labour and the London Poor* by Henry Mayhew. It's fantastic journalism, a brilliant study of real-life Victorian crossing-sweepers, costermongers and vagrants full of heart-breaking personal details. All it takes is a good book to transport yourself into another world. We meet Lola for our daily walk round the park.

Monday March 23
Lockdown begins and it's Nicola's birthday. She's having to make do with my home-made card, the thermal base layer I bought her and some chocolates, as everything else is shut. Lola and Michael come over and stand in the garden, while Nell is socially-distanced at the top of the stairs and we're in the kitchen. This would make a great Samuel Beckett play if we could just bury someone up to their neck. We share Earl Grey tea and birthday cake. Nicola cooks an anti-consumerist birthday dinner of a broad bean stew and loves it, declaring this to be one of her best ever birthdays.

Tuesday March 24
There's a sack of wood on our doorstep. The Wood Man has returned! Clearly he thinks that the most helpful thing he can do for lockdown is to give us plenty of firewood. Inside the builder's sack he's deposited are various pieces of curved darker wood, bits of decking, weathered pieces of garden fence, small bits of ply, numerous off-cuts and lots of sawdust. It turns out Nicola met him in the street a month ago and sort-of said he could give us some more

wood.

The Wood Man is an active green and has been building structures for a guerrilla park that he plans to install on a piece of local wasteground. Recently his house caught fire, but it was luckily extinguished before his extensive supplies of wood ignited and our road became the 2020 equivalent of Pudding Lane. I take the sack of wood down to the cellar. We might struggle for loo rolls, food and PPE, but as things fall apart we shall never be short of wood.

My AdSense account has made one pence today. Nell compiles a quarantine playlist on Spotify including *The End of the World As We Know It* by REM, *Stayin' Alive* by the Bee Gees, *Isolation* by Joy Division and *Don't Stand So Close To Me* by the Police. Do some more music biographies before an email arrives to say the office is closing and the writers are unemployed until lockdown ends. I make sure I finish all my seven biographies for the week and send off an invoice in the hope they'll pay quickly. At the moment it looks like the Pilates newsletter will still be going out even if the studio is closed, though my book projects aren't going to get very far with publishers in the present uncertain climate.

Meanwhile scaffolders are erecting scaffolding outside our house. A couple of months ago we'd booked a roofing company to finally replace our rotting soffits and they insist they still want to do the job. We offer the men a cup of tea, place it on the doorstep and run inside.

We go onto something called Zoom and establish a link with our friend Nicky, who is self-isolated and alone in Shepherd's Bush. It's important to get the lighting good and have a glass of wine to hand as we establish a video link. Zoom soon becomes the tool of choice for people to tell each other how bored or not they are, though Nicky seems fine, even if the death figures are mounting on the BBC *News*.

Wednesday March 25
Having watched endless episodes of *Doctor Who* I can get through this. We're only allowed out for one hour's exercise a day. The deserted streets of Islington remind me of the start of *The Dalek Invasion of Earth*, where the Doctor, Ian, Barbara and Susan walk through the empty streets of a once-bustling London and come across a poster saying, "It is forbidden to dump bodies in to the river". Ian immediately wonders if there has been a plague. *The Survivors* terrified me as a kid and later came more dystopian films, *A Clockwork Orange*, *Mad Max*, *28 Days Later*. Psychologically my life of screen viewing should perhaps have prepared me for the real apocalypse.

Am I risking my life buying some bagels? Bread is proving problematic now Salt The Radish the local café that sells Hippy Bread has shut. The bagel shop has taped off most of its interior and is selling bagels from the door. People in masks are queuing at two-metres distances outside Lidl, making it all look like some weird episode of *Doctor Who.*

Work on writing up our trip to Grasmere for my proposed Lake District book on bagging Wainwrights. That will be five chapters done with 59 fells left to complete. But who knows when I will ever get to complete them? But writing is what I do, and lockdown allows us all to concentrate on what matters.

The sink isn't draining in the bathroom. So I take out the stash of Who Gives A Crap? loo rolls from under the sink, plus a toilet bag full of hundreds of old toothbrushes that Nicola has kept for some reason, and remove the u-bend. It's horrible. I pull out balls of grey slime, consisting of hair, shaving foam, bristles and general thermonuclear gunk. When I replace the u-bend the washer on the joint snaps. There's a big leak without a waterproof seal.

So I go to see Mrs Lu at the local hardware shop and get another washer for 50p. Only it proves to be too big. Return to the shop and discover that it's closed, and is only open from 11am-1pm in lockdown. So have to cordon off the sink with piles of loo roll and toilet bags with instructions not to use it until tomorrow when I should be able to get another washer. Cross plumber off my list of possible alternative careers.

After dinner I find Nicola in her office watching a film on paddle-boarding while standing on her wobble cushion and paddling with a broomstick. This seems entirely normal.

Thursday March 26
"Bloody fox!" I'm in my dressing gown having opened the front door and am now surveying two milk bottles on their sides, with the foil caps removed. Clearly the fox was thirsty, but did it have to knock over both bottles? Doesn't it know there's a pandemic on? It's left an inch of milk at the bottom of each pint, no doubt now contaminated by foxy diseases. To add to my distress, the milkman has left a bill, which includes the two pints of milk that we will now never drink.

Visit the hardware shop at 11am and manage to replace the washer on the bathroom sink. Brave the queue at Sainsbury's. Only three shoppers are allowed in at once and the temptation is to race round doing a big weekly shop. I stock up on sausages, chicken Kiev for Nell, hummus, cheese, mushrooms, peanuts, beer and other N4 essentials. Finish the last section of my Grasmere chapter, which all feels like a different world now. Nell is out of isolation today and able to eat with us.

Chancellor Rishi Sunak has announced measures to

help the self-employed from June, allowing them to claim 80 per cent of their profits from the government. But as my profit after expenses was only £400 last year, that isn't going to be much, even if I'm entitled to it.

My afternoon's work is disturbed by the drama in the street outside. The street-corner drug dealing is becoming a lot more obvious without passers-by. Four plain-clothes policeman have drawn up in their car to deal with a user who is possibly overdosing. They negotiate with his friend while the addict staggers around the empty street, spiralling and swaying and looking like he should be at Woodstock. "Tell him to put his clothes on!" suggests one officer. The man is now throwing off his lime green trainers. Eventually the two druggies shuffle off and the police car departs. Half an hour later the overdoser returns and a neighbour attempts to see him off with a yapping dog.

He's back again though and decides to lie down on the pavement outside our garden hedge. A police car full of uniformed officers turns up and also an ambulance. The prone figure is surrounded by six people in uniform all wearing plastic gloves. He says he's just sleeping. After twenty minutes of negotiations it's decided that an ambulance is not required and the police instruct the druggie to move away from the vicinity. He moves off to bring further mayhem somewhere else. You've got to feel sorry for someone so dependant and out of it, though the whole scenario brings a dystopian feel to our street. If this were *Fahrenheit 451* the user would be frisked for books, particularly those by Pete May.

But in the evening our neighbourhood returns to being like Bedford Falls in *It's a Wonderful Life*. There's a big noise in the street at eight o'clock as everyone stands on their doorsteps and applauding and banging saucepans to salute the NHS workers who are treating coronavirus patients and in the process risking their own lives.

We watch *Friday Night Dinner* on catch-up as recommended by Nell, though it's obviously nothing like our family. "Oh yes it is," says Nell, as dad Martin obsessively tries to remove a plastic bag from a tree with a rake device and in another episode conceals the dead fox he's keeping in the freezer.

Friday March 27
Nicola wakes up with a scream, having dreamt that she had a worm in her hand — her ultimate nightmare — after first being chased by ghost dogs. There's probably a whole conference in this. Lockdown seems to be causing a lot of people to have bad dreams.

KDP tells me I've sold an e-book of *Man About Tarn,* making a profit of £1.72. It's selling one a day this week and getting more Kindle Unlimited page reads, so perhaps having a captive audience is helping. My KDP books have earned nearly £50 this month, though a global pandemic wasn't quite what I had in mind to boost sales.

The roofers are soon busy up the scaffolding tearing down our crumbling old soffits, which seem to consist of wattle and daub. We give them tea, retrieve the cups and wash them up carefully in hot water with soap.

Lola WhatsApps our Family Bonding group to say that Boris Johnson has coronavirus. Which doesn't seem that surprising as he's a politician and was boasting about still shaking hands with everyone on March 3, though he did advocate washing hands and singing 'Happy Birthday' while doing so. So the country is now leaderless.

The *Guardian* has just had a top ten of Tom Hanks films and we watch *Apollo 13*, a film about the ultimate isolation of being stuck in space and almost never returning.

Saturday March 28

Go to the Deli at 80 and join the socially-distanced queue on the pavement. I discover that they are still selling Bread by Bike's Hippy Bread, recently voted the best bread in the country, which is a result. Walking through the back streets it seems that some things are getting better with lockdown. The traffic is at 1950s levels and I can walk in the road with impunity. Bird song is in the air. And Vulcan isn't finding chicken bones at every tree pit. Another bonus is that our local foxes are not finding so much street refuse and depositing it in our garden.

One mistake I have made is not to get a haircut before lockdown. Nicola decides to trim the hair above my ears

"It's ok, I know how to cut hair, I've cut the feathers of my horse."

"So that obviously qualifies you to be a barber? And I didn't know horses had feathers."

"It will be fine!" she says with the confidence of someone who has her own specially-trained pony.

She first trawls through my greying hair with a nit comb, a remnant of primary school infestations. We can't find any other comb, apart from the one we use for the dog.

"This won't hurt," she says.

"That's what Sweeney Todd said," I reply.

"Sssh. I'm concentrating!"

"Ow, you're putting the scissors in my ear! I expect Van Gogh probably let his wife cut his hair and that didn't turn out well…"

Actually, apart from some painful nit combing, Nicola does a pretty good job trimming above my ears. Though at some stage I need to find some clippers and get to work on the back and top of my Barnet.

Meanwhile the soffit men continue to saw up fibre

glass and add the special holes for swifts that Nicola has requested, much to their bemusement. Nell is feeling nihilistic as her first year at university has been ruined and it's supposed to be the best years of her life. We tell her that at least she's healthy and things will improve. We enjoyed life after university too and what doesn't kill you only makes you stronger.

At the five o'clock press conference deputy PM Dominic Raab brings more sobering news that the death toll from coronavirus has now reached a thousand. Nell cooks us veggie meatballs with spaghetti, which improves everyone's spirits. Then we watch Michael Portillo travelling by train through Canada on the TV. I remember travel, it was big in 2019.

Sunday March 29
Start to read *War and Peace* in the garden. We might be entombed in Finsbury Park but within these pages I'm in Moscow and St Petersburg at the height of the Napoleonic wars. Imagining myself to be Pierre Bezukhov or maybe Levin in *Anna Karenin*, I try to find solace in manual labour, chopping some firewood in the garden, sawing up some planks the Wood Man left us and clearing out the cellar, sorting out bags of dusty kindling.

The soffit men are taking a break and Nicola is in a paint-spattered hoodie on the scaffolding painting the windows. I would help her were it not for vertigo and general uselessness. There's a worrying gap, where the scaffolding is only two planks wide and protected by just one rail. Nicola doesn't look that confident either.

"Can you hold this darling... I mean Pete..." she says, passing me a tin of cream paint.

"You called me darling, you must be terrified..."

Monday March 30

The subsidence men arrive to take the latest readings from the studs in the walls of our house. They keep a discreet two metres from us as we open up the door to the back garden. Our home continues to slowly rise and fall with the turbid ebb and flow of human misery — and the movement of London clay. Covid-19 will be long gone by the time a judgement is reached on our case.

Do some work on the April edition of the Pilates newsletter, finding the news that Pilates advocate and former Green Goddess Diana Moran is now taking a fitness class on the BBC's *Good Morning*. Prepare my accounts. This year it looks like my turnover will be just over £8000. That's not much to most people, but it's a vast improvement on the previous year's turnover of £2600. Having the regular music biographies and latterly the Pilates newsletter has helped, along with the wellness app ghost-writing and PR work. Only this coming year it's going to plummet again with most of the staff in the UK furloughed, newspapers and magazines becoming thinner with each day and publishers unlikely to commit to new books by mid or rather low-list writers like me. Not that this matters that much when people are dying.

As the industry has contracted my horizons have got smaller, but now it's happening to everyone. The media is full of alarmed articles about how to survive working at home, or how to cope in self-isolation. Writers have been self-isolating for years. We have some of the qualities of resilience needed to get through this and we're used to surviving on little money. My world is now this house.

The soffit men finish their work and head off for new roofs. The new soffits include holes for swifts. Nicola has a memory stick of the song of the swift, which she puts in a borrowed black box device, with a wire attached to a small speaker that's outside our bedroom window. Tweets start echoing around our bedroom. "We just play this every morning and evening, the song will help attract the swifts, they like to go where there are other swifts," she explains. "I'm not sure this is the sort of twitter feed I wanted," I suggest. "It's now like sleeping in a human nest."

Tuesday March 31
Let the chickens out, then walk Vulcan. Read the *Guardian*. The death figures are heading towards 2000, and it's not just the elderly who are dying. Hospital staff are struggling to get adequate protection gear.

Transfer my half of the £4k fee for replacing the soffits. Savings are vital now. We're lucky. Owning a house is expensive, but at least we do own it. If we still had a mortgage or were renting we'd be pretty desperate like millions of other people.

The homeless are struggling now no-one carries cash and no takeaways are open. Jules, one of Nicola's homeless readers of *The Pavement* arrives to charge his phone. He stays at a discreet distance in the garden. We give him a stool and offer him refreshment as he lights a joss stick and places it in a flower pot. He opts for Earl Grey tea with honey and sourdough toast with jam. When the phone is charged he sets off for his daughter's house and gives us a present of some Donald Trump loo paper and a joss stick. Then it's back to the screen of my Mac. What will words be worth in the post-Covid-19 age? The last year and a bit has been a struggle followed by a contagion.

Newspapers are getting thinner and thinner and there are endless journalists writing about lockdown. I'm not sure journalism is a viable option anymore. Book writing just might be, if the publishers survive. Perhaps self-publishing is a way to get to get some product out into the market, should I survive the plague year. Maybe a publisher will remember some of my other books and take a gamble. But these things are out of my control. This is going to be about resilience – and perhaps freelancers are quite good at it.

Most of the country is now depending on the government to pay their wages. Companies are folding and unemployment is soaring. A massive recession is on the way. People have stopped wearing smart clothes to work and become scruffs, slumping in tattered walking trousers and old fleeces, as freelancers always have done. We're all skint and isolated now. But what I do know is that once you start writing you don't give up. I'm going to be isolated for months thanks to a pandemic that no-one expected in the modern age. No distractions now, no excuses. This nobody is going to write his diary.

ALSO BY PETE MAY

Man About Tarn

Goodbye to Boleyn

Whovian Dad

The Joy of Essex

World Cup Expert: Teams

World Cup Expert: Players

Flying So High: West Ham's Cup Finals

There's A Hippo In My Cistern

Hammers In the Heart

Ageing Body, Confused Mind

Football and its Followers

Rent Boy

West Ham: Irons in the Soul

Sunday Muddy Sunday

The Lad Done Bad

Printed in Great Britain
by Amazon

61319178R00119